SPRING TROUT & STRAWBERRY PANCAKES

SPRING TROUT & STRAWBERRY PANCAKES

Borrowed Tales, Quirky Cures, Camp Recipes and the Adirondack Characters Who Cooked Them Up

STORIES AND RECIPES WITH A DISTINCT WOODLAND FLAVOR

NOT YOUR ORDINARY COOKBOOK

William J. O'Hern

The book and cover design and typesetting
were created by Nancy Did It! (www.NancyDidIt.com)

Words from "Mountain Air" is used by permission
© 1987 Dan Berggren/Berggren Music, BMI.
Grateful acknowledgement is made to www.berggrenfolk.com.

Grateful acknowledgement is made to Richard Nadeau
of Moose River Trading Co. in Thendara, NY, for the use of his
"Guide's at a Campfire" illustration for the chapter title pages.

In the Adirondacks

Camden, New York • www.adkwilds.com

Printed in the United States of America by Versa Press, Inc.
ISBN 978-0-9890328-4-1

CONTENTS

Preface

Author's Note

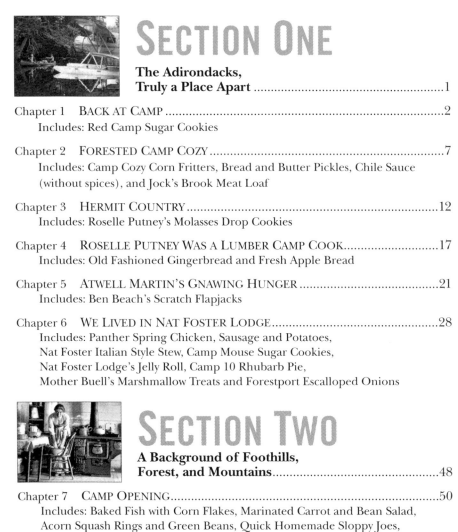

SECTION ONE

The Adirondacks, Truly a Place Apart

SECTION TWO

A Background of Foothills, Forest, and Mountains

SECTION THREE

**People and
Places** 100

SECTION FOUR

A Treasury of Timeless Tales and Trail-tested Recipes 149

SECTION FIVE

PREFACE

I'VE OFTEN THOUGHT that if time travel were possible, I would journey back to the old-time Adirondack camps of the early 20th century. It would be enough of a thrill to meet some backwoods characters and citified sports and listen to their everyday stories and time-honored tall tales. Better yet would be to enjoy the aroma of freshly-caught trout frying in a cast iron skillet, knowing that in moments I'd be tasting that crispy camp standby—an entrée sought out and savored by countless Adirondack enthusiasts for hundreds of years.

I've visited many of the old camps as they are now, and kibitzed with old-timers. I've thumbed through camp journals and cookbooks and fingered through the pages of vintage photo albums.

Surviving records and snapshots of those who enjoyed rustic shelters and old-time cabins now rest as dreamless dust. The old log buildings sited along lakeshores and rivers and scattered throughout the woods are gone, as are roadside campsite pull-offs. But the old stories and scenes survive, frozen in time on yellowed and stained photographic paper, and one can still imagine the sound of the steel wagon wheel rim or iron horseshoe gong that once rang loud across water and traveled through the trees: "Return to camp! It's time to eat!" and perhaps later, "Listen to a tale or two."

Food is an innate part of every culture, and nearly everyone has a stash of Grandma's secret recipes that appear on holidays or simply for nostalgia's sake. Inventive problem-solving has always been part of camp culture for those who'd rather innovate than waste a half-day's good fishing going to town. Camp recipes and inventions for everything from alleviating indigestion to warding off black flies were topics of everyday conversation in the old camps.

Many of these treasured camp recipes and remedies are just as good as ever today, and an old-time tale told by a campfire or woodstove is now perhaps better than ever because of its novelty. So just for a while, forget the latest celebrity chef, side-effect-laden pharmaceuticals, and television drama. Join me for a taste of the old days and old ways. While time travel remains only a dream, the voices of the Adirondacks' past can still be heard by the astute reader of *Spring Trout & Strawberry Pancakes: Borrowed Tails, Quirky Cures, Camp Recipes and the Adirondack Characters Who Cook Them Up.*

No classier woodland camp could be asked for by the ladies and men during the 1890s. *Courtesy Bill Zullo, Hamilton County Historian*

AUTHOR'S NOTE

I SHAKE MY HEAD in amazement when I think of the freedom I enjoyed as a child at my once rural home and those times spent at Camp Oasis on the Seneca River, my grandparents' riverfront retreat. To this day I marvel at my parents' and grandparents' trust in my judgment and at the lack of restraint on my movement.

I grew up in what I've heard some city people call The Sticks—farms, expansive pastures, meadows and woodland—acres upon acres of undeveloped land. To me it was all wild beauty, a keystone of my youth. Like one friend and contributor to this work, Roy Wires, I grew up wild and free, often walking the fields in bare feet. There wasn't a place I couldn't go as long as I had a knapsack of food, a .22 rifle and a fishing pole. Roy and I played with cousins and friends who lived in the city, but there was always something about the urban setting that made us feel we didn't fit in.

My connection to the countryside always reminded me of a certain Little Golden Book, *The Country Mouse and the City Mouse.* We'd rather have been catching box turtles and stalking the wild pheasants. The creeks were clear and the shoreline perfect for lounging after we piled up rocks to support our poles; all we needed to do was watch for the red and white bobber to dip below the surface of the water.

Today, our former country setting has heavily suffered the plight of suburban sprawl. Creeks are diverted through drainage culverts; housing developments have replaced meadows. There is a series of apartment houses where I once caught pollywogs, and now the nearby "Sherwood Forest" is not a forest at all, but a subdivision street that ends in a cul-de-sac.

I recall only a single warning about people I didn't know. *Don't trust strangers.* The majority of instructions regarding safety in my daily life and wanderings were about important matters like how to properly use a jack knife, a hatchet, a rowboat and later a boat powered by an outboard motor.

Many early childhood swimming instructions abounded. Living in proximity to a water world required me to learn how to swim well. Safety was of the utmost importance. I began swimming wearing the typical flotation device of the day—a ring of brightly colored balsa floats connected by a belt strapped around my waist. By the age of five or six I was swimming unaided.

Being able to swim allowed me the privilege of taking the wooden rowboat out on the water alone. Grandpa was the manager of the Potter Boat Company. We always had a number of rowboats and motorboats moored by the docks.

In 1957, I earned the privilege of taking a small motorboat beyond the boundaries of the river and into the lake. Demonstrating that I had learned proper boat safety was an important step. It meant I was allowed to go beyond sight of the dock, either up or down river.

Camp Oasis, June 1947. My grandparents worked on their camp for years to bring it up to its prime. Deer and rabbits were all over the place, and I slept in the attic with the sound of bull frogs calling from the swamp across the river. *Author's Collection*

Just six months shy of my twelfth birthday; I had demonstrated my proficiency with the 7½ horsepower Evinrude outboard motor. Up until that time I would be given permission to drive the small power boat only when an adult was with me. My exploring range expanded that year.

In most respects my grandparents were conventional camp owners, and in some ways they were not. Grandma arrived in America in 1896 at the age of five with her mother, father and two sisters. Her mother and father emigrated from England. My grandfather's parents had also immigrated to this country from Switzerland, in 1895.

Grandma and Grandpa Zysset were in a motorcycle group. They enjoyed hill climbing. They also took long motorcycle trips throughout the North Country and the Adirondacks. They were handy. Grandpa was a carpenter,

Bette and Kerry O'Hern enjoy a noontime break as the author tells an Adirondack tale.
Photograph by author

Spring Trout & Strawberry Pancakes: Borrowed Tales, Quirky Cures, Camp Recipes

mechanic and jack of all trades; Grandma could rebuild a canoe, lay up a cobblestone wall, weave rugs out of rags and accomplish just about any other handicraft. She was also an excellent cook and baker.

Their goal was to retire and live out their days at camp, where they would continue to raise the majority of their food. Camp Oasis's setting and my parents' rural home location proved to be the matrix that exposed me to the satisfaction that comes with work and to the joys of being outdoors.

Trees and plants, water and boats, dragonflies, butterflies, birds, frogs and turtles, Grandma's yeast bread, listening to people who effortlessly told stories, and learning to appreciate all things in nature enriched my life. Lessons in using tools and inpracticality were also important. If there had been the array of entertaining electronic devices we have today, I wonder if I would have turned out the same.

I attribute the experiences of my youth to my appreciation of Adirondack history and my love of the Adirondack Park. Not wanting to neglect those mothers and grandmothers who baked wonderful dishes that are so different from today's and those fathers and grandfathers who told gripping stories and supplied their families with income from logging, guiding, farming, carpentry and masonry, to name only a few of the occupations Adirondack folks relied on for their economic survival, I've woven this eclectic collection of profiles and tales, recipes and home cures, along with a vast number of early Adirondack camp photos.

Today's sprawling suburban road systems make me more and more thankful for the visionaries who created the Adirondack Park. The whole pioneer life of the region is fascinating to me. The history of this and that Adirondack county, the guides and early settlers are etched in my bones— hard men and women, hard times, but fascinating social history.

Adirondack Spring Trout & Strawberry Pancakes: Camp Recipes, Quirky Cures and the Adirondack Characters Who Cook Them Up is my opportunity to tap into that lore—into the part of history that explores the not-so-common lives and ways of everyday Adirondack campers, something that has always been a fascination for me. Perhaps you will discover something amusing, useful or just plain interesting that you won't find anywhere else. 🎋

1947. "Out on the water." The very words bring to mind a mood, a feeling, an image of a scene where both paddlers and passengers aboard Harold Scott's float plane could relax and enjoy cool Adirondack scenes. Photographer: Gene Badger. *Courtesy Town of Webb Historical Association*

The Adirondacks, Truly a Place Apart

"It was the magnificent scenery that attracted visitors to the North Country, just as it had enticed people to reside there in years gone by. The natural grandeur of the wooded mountains with their rounded peaks, the breath-taking beauty of the lakes and streams spelled relaxation of a unique nature. Invigorating summer weather lured the visitor to sandy beaches, refreshing plunges in the quiet waters, rowing on the deep-blue lakes that cut deep into forested land. There was the joy of hiking over leaf-covered mountain trails, the sight of the graceful agile deer. Fishing in abundance or rewarding hunting for the sportsman was a further lure." —Ted Aber, *Adirondack Folks*

CHAPTER 1

Back at Camp

"An uneventful day at camp save a brief call by "Joe" Jenkins, the state game warden, accompanied by a young man named Yerdon and another warden. They were looking for Fred Owen and a Roberts of the Red Camp party for killing a doe. I am sorry if Mr. Owen is in trouble, for he is a good man."—Rev. A. L. Byron-Curtiss, Nat Foster Lodge Log Book, Nov. 14, 1933

THE RED CAMP was a cheery-looking place that for many years had known the gentle touch of George Hoxie's attentive handyman skills. Once, it was a rambling, squatty, out-of-square building with hand-split cedar shingles fashioned by native Owen "Kettle" Jones. Jones came by his nickname from making a wild berry brandy-of-sorts in his mountain still. Hoxie enjoyed telling tales about hermit Kettle and his pet raccoon's fondness for the homemade brew, which they shared in the backwoods beyond Hoxie's place. George and all who used the camp loved the Adirondacks.

A dirt dogtrot connected Red Camp to Drs. Jones-Fuller Camp and the Wiggins Camp, and on to Nat Foster Lodge, along North Lake's shoreline.

The Red Camp's porch roof shaded and sheltered those who rocked on the plank porch below, perhaps wrapped in a light robe against the morning chill, as they watched the warming morning rays of the sun burn off wisps of fog that draped over the lake's surface. During the day, campers gathered to do nothing other than to relax, nibble camp-standard cookies and enjoy being at a much-beloved location—the lakeside.

Harold McNitt was the senior partner of Red Camp. As a boy, McNitt was called a "whippersnapper" in what he believes was the best sense of the word. Rev. Byron-Curtiss, a close adult friend who lived at Nat Foster Lodge, assured him it was a term of endearment. McNitt had been coming to North Lake since 1922. He said he had never missed a year.

"Call me Nitty," he instructed me as he introduced himself. We were sitting in the shade on the porch, and it was the summer of 1996. As we shared bits about our background I learned the camp had been his woodland home since he was a young child. "I've baked some cookies. Come into the cabin kitchen," he motioned. We continued our chat by an old-looking wood cook stove, surrounded by spic-and-span wood-paneled walls that had been painted white.

Sitting at a century-old kitchen table, Harold closed his eyes and recited this simple poem he had written.

North Lake, My Treasure
"The ducks will always visit North Lake camps for bread.
Every day the loons will sing their magical phrases
And sometimes do their dances by Blueberry Island.
For every year the magic of North Lake,
The most beautiful place on earth,
Sends out its magnets to draw its real lovers back."

I immediately liked Nitty. He and his camp buddies play a part in the true story of the history of the backwoods of Atwell, New York.

I had come to learn about Nitty's family connection with the so-called "Bishop of North Lake," the Reverend Arthur Leslie Byron-Curtiss. I was researching the Episcopalian minister's life for a biography.[1]

"The Reverend stayed over there (*Harold pointed with his finger.*) for months. He was often the sole inhabitant on this side of the lake. There were only a few camps over there in the cove. Byron-Curtiss walked a lot. He enjoyed it. I remember him always clean and neatly dressed. His clothing never smelled smoky. He wore serviceable North Woods attire. He was an affable person, a man you liked being around as a kid. I went over to his camp often. He told lots of stories; we often talked fishing.

"Once I earned ten dollars. There was a party of men drinking over there. They had cases of beer. Whiskey bottles were everywhere. So, too, were many cans of pipe tobacco and Sweet Cuba chewing plugs. They weren't in much of a climate to clean the bullheads they had caught. One fella asked me if I'd do it for them. I didn't mind helping. Besides, I knew The Reverend would include me in the group's fish fry. I got me a log, took a nail, drove it with a hammer right through the fishes' heads, cut the back fin right off and skinned them outright. Well! Much to my great surprise 'B-C,' as he liked to be called, proposed they pick up a collection for me. One dollar was a lot of money back in those days, so you can imagine the value of ten dollars—a small fortune!

"The McNitts were singers, good ones. Sometimes we sang on the porch. I often joined in. If you were out on the water you could have heard us at Mayhew Cove. 'Course everything is so quiet up here, voices carry across the water clearly."

Nitty was neither a guide nor native woodsman, but I found him to be a natural outdoorsman and someone who thoroughly enjoyed camp life. His cheerful humor, his resourcefulness, his knack for remembering yarns, and his complete accord with the serenity of nature helped me understand how thoroughly imbued he was with the woods and waters and how the Adirondacks had influenced his growth throughout the years.

Nitty also baked rich, tasty fundamental cookies, a weakness of mine I fight because they are loaded with saturated fat and cholesterol—a fact Nitty quipped made them "honest to goodness baking. That's why they taste so good." Nitty's recipe is simple:

Recipe   **RED CAMP SUGAR COOKIES**

2 cups sugar.
1 rounded cup of butter.
4 eggs.
4 teaspoons baking powder.
4 cups pastry flour.
Vanilla.
Roll, cut and bake.

"Camp Mayhew became the 'Red Camp' on August 20, 1972, the date the faded white clapboard siding was painted red." —Harold McNitt. Adirondack porches are places to relax and enjoy a cool breeze on a warm night—a place for eating, reading, rocking, and storytelling. *Courtesy Meredith Flerlage*

Nitty said his grandmother had taught him to make cookies, pies and biscuits as well as other things. Nitty had thought about having a little camp garden, but would have had to fight off the critters. He liked to hang his laundry to dry on lines stretched between trees in the fresh mountain air.

We stood side-by-side at the white-enameled sink and looked at old snapshots tacked on the wall. He pointed out a picture of himself as a young kid.

Once, when he was cutting shapes in sugar cookie dough his grandmother had rolled out, she told him a baking secret: rum doesn't count as alcohol if it's drenching your fruit cake.

Nitty enjoyed living off the grid in a turn-of-the-20th-century Adirondack cottage complete with a canoe, a rowboat and a boat with a small outboard engine. He drew water from a spring, bucket by bucket, and used a bucksaw and sawhorse to work up wood for fuel. It was an idyllic mountain-spun life. Inspired by those pioneer years, his ancestors, and the elderly Atwell natives, he'd spent a lifetime learning about old-timey ways, backwoods cooking, common wisdom and tall tales. 🍵

Harold McNitt, far right, with his uncles, taken at the foot of North Lake.
Courtesy Harold McNitt

CHAPTER 2

Forested Camp Cozy

NITTY'S RED CAMP, Nat Foster Lodge and Camp Cozy were three of many sites tucked back in the foothills of the Adirondacks, in Atwell at the headwaters of the Black River. A range of treed-over low mountains separates Atwell from the Fulton Chain.

"My husband and I never considered we needed a classier cabin than Cozy for our honeymoon retreat," said Emily Mitchell Wires when thinking about her family's Adirondack camp. "Camp Cozy's atmosphere provided experiences which contributed to my physical growth and character development. It lingers long in my memory." When Emily Wires wrote these words in 1966, she set a scene familiar and near to the heart of everyone who grew up or vacationed in the Adirondacks. Emily described Camp Cozy as having "a level of comfort above the bare necessities of existence."

"Back at camp…" The very words bring to mind a mood, a feeling, an image of a place to relax and enjoy a cool breeze on a warm night, a place from which to explore, for reading, rocking, cooking and storytelling.

Emily was not the first to find restoration of health and growth of character in a rugged, outdoor existence, but she was one of few who have had the creative ability and descriptive power to make such an experience valuable and stimulating to her grandson, Roy E. Wires.

Emily's legacy is not restricted to a camp diary, recipe book and a box of memorabilia. She told her grandson she was grateful to her grandparents, for her parents' stories and to the old-timers who were responsible for turning her outdoor life into a storybook populated by the locals who lived robustly in the Black River country.

Emily and Edwin Wires at Camp Cozy. *Courtesy Roy E. Wires (The Emily Mitchell Wires Collection)*

Spring Trout & Strawberry Pancakes: Borrowed Tales, Quirky Cures, Camp Recipes

Emily was often in the company of her sisters, and the girls became knowledgeable about resident animals and birds, learned to identify trees by their bark patterns, fished and enjoyed helping prepare camp meals. She rated herself as good at fishing and cooking, but a poor markswoman.

No matter how good your screens were or how hard you tried, it was impossible to keep all the flies out of the camp, particularly in the fall, when the weather began to grow cold and the old kitchen smelled so nicely of canning, pickling, and cooking. "We used an old method learned from our grandparents to fight flies," said Emily. "We'd take the stiff paper of a flour sack, cut it into strips, tie the strips to a stick or part of a broom handle. Then with several of these weapons, we would open the door and, starting from the back part of the room, flail the air vigorously until we had chased the flies out."

Then too there were the old-fashioned sticky sheets of fly paper that were hung from the ceiling. They caught their share of flies, and an unsuspecting girl's hair too.

Recipe CAMP COZY CORN FRITTERS

A fast, easy and filling camp meal.
1 cup cream corn; 1 egg, beaten; 2 rounded tablespoons flour;
2 rounded tablespoons baking powder; Pinch of salt.
Directions: To egg add corn. Next, add sifted dry ingredients.
Fry like pancakes and serve with maple syrup.

Emily said she always brought jars of pickles and sauce to camp. Her pickles and sauce recipes are labeled "from Ma Wires."

Recipe BREAD & BUTTER PICKLES

7 quarts cucumbers, peeled and sliced thin.
1 quart sliced onions.
6 green peppers, sliced.
¼ cup white mustard seed.
1 teaspoon Turmeric.
2 teaspoons salt.
6 cups sugar.

1½ quarts vinegar.

Directions: Soak cucumbers and onions and peppers in salt water over night. Put sugar, mustard seed, turmeric, vinegar and salt in kettle. Let come to a boil. Drop in onions, peppers, and cucumbers. Let come to boil again and seal in jars.

Recipe | **CHILE SAUCE** (without spices)

12 tomatoes, peeled and cut up.

Grind together:

4 green peppers.

4 onions.

1 cup sugar.

1 cup vinegar added at end of cooking.

2 teaspoons salt.

Camp Cozy, circa 1918. *Courtesy Roy E. Wires (The Emily Mitchell Wires Collection)*

Spring Trout & Strawberry Pancakes: Borrowed Tales, Quirky Cures, Camp Recipes

Mulchy Spring, a.k.a Whiskey Spring, was along the road to North Lake. Emily's youthful party often stopped to eat lunch and drink the truly delicious water. The stopover was also an opportunity to spoof for the camera. *Courtesy George Shaughnessy*

Recipe   **JOCK'S BROOK MEAT LOAF**

Emily's husband swore he could smell the aroma
of this dish clear across the lake.

1 slightly beaten egg.

1 lb. ground beef.

½ lb. ground pork.

½ cup cracker crumbs.

1 small onion chopped.

1 tablespoon horseradish.

1 tablespoon ketchup.

1 tablespoon green pepper chopped.

1½ teaspoon salt.

1 cup scalded milk.

Directions: Combine egg and meat. Mix other ingredients with scalded milk. Add to meat. Press into loaf pan. Bake 350°F. in oven one hour.

CHAPTER 3

Hermit Country

NORTH LAKE was hermit country, Nitty told.

I wasn't unaware of that fact.

I'd heard many stories about the hermit Atwell Martin and his phenomenal appetite from my friend Roy Wires. Roy's grandmother, Emily Mitchell Wires, used to tell Roy all about Martin, who was her father's guide. He was famous for his ability to eat enormous quantities of food. Nitty's and some other locals' tales—some fanciful, others legendary—bring the hermit-guide's life alive.

Lore has it that Atwell did not enjoy eating his own cooking. Hearsay also said Atwell ate at irregular times, although he would be the first to tell someone he liked "regular meals."

What whetted his appetite more than anything else was someone else's cooking. Emily remembers stories about Mrs. Roselle Putney of Forestport. She used to be the cook at Gideon Perry's Number Two logging camp. Atwell frequently appeared at the cook house. He claimed Putney's molasses drop cookies were the best in the land.

A note in Emily's Camp Cozy cookbook reveals that her formula is an old recipe passed down. I believe it had to have been Roselle Putney's original lumber camp recipe.

Recipe **ROSELLE PUTNEY'S MOLASSES DROP COOKIES**

1½ cups sugar.

1 cup lard or Crisco.

3 unbeaten eggs (Save some egg white with
which to glaze tops of cookies before baking).
½ cup molasses.
3½ cups sifted bread flour .
1 cup raisins & ½ cup nut meats.
1 teaspoon each of cloves, cinnamon, allspice, soda, salt.
Directions: Cream Crisco, sugar & salt. Add spices, then eggs—
one at a time. Next add raisins & molasses; lastly flour sifted
with soda. Drop & flatten; brush with slightly beaten egg. Bake
5 to 7 minutes in 325°F. oven.

Emily added this afterthought: *These cookies are very rich & tops
should be left slightly soft in baking.*

Following Putney's stint as logging camp cook, she was hired sometime in
the early 1890s by Ed Klock's wife. Ed was the North Lake reservoir custo-
dian, and Mrs. Putney served as a cook and domestic helper at the State
House. Atwell, who lived across from the State House[2], always stood by her
when she was putting up the lunches for parties he was hired to guide,
watching, hoping and often asking in his falsetto voice if she was going to
be packing this or that into the tin lunch pails.

Atwell tales added to Nitty's and Emily's love affairs with mountain life.
The recluse's life is worth recapping, for Atwell Martin had a weakness for
fishing and strawberries.

Lore tells a woman was responsible for sending Martin to the woods and
making a hermit out of him in the 1850s.

Byron Cool, who knew Atwell best, related this profile to Harvey L. Dunham, a commercial artist and collector of Adirondack lore.

"Atwell Martin was born in a log cabin on the woods side of Baker Brook,
near Remsen and grew up there," Cool told Dunham. "Then young Atwell
fell head-over-heels in love with a girl who decided she didn't like him.
That stunned Atwell.

"Most young men would have picked up another girl and forgotten their
broken hearts, but not Atwell. He was different. It drove him to the tall
timber, where he landed at North Lake.

North Lake hermit Atwell Martin. *Courtesy of the Maitland C. DeSormo Collection*

"That was not long after the Civil War, and sore beset, he wandered aimlessly about the woods for a long time, always getting back one day or another to North Lake. The gal was with him all the time—in his mind.

"Atwell wanted to build a shack to live in, so Byron Cool hauled several logs from the foot of the lake to Reed's Mill, a few miles down the tote road toward Forestport, and when the logs had been sawed, he hauled the lumber back. Atwell nailed together this little board wigwam in which he lived for many years.

"A flood carried away the dam at North Lake.[3] Then the state built a bigger and better one. It had another dam several miles north at Canachagala Lake 'on top of a mountain,' as they used to say, and a third dam several miles south on Twin Lakes.

"The state thought it had better have a gate tender to regulate the flow of water for the Black River Canal, and there was Atwell Martin on the spot, ready to take the job. It suited him precisely, for he had slowed down in his wanderings and tending dam gates didn't interfere much with his 'settin',' which had become quite a pastime.

"Moreover, the state offered to pay him $1,800 per year, which was a stupendous wage for the [18]70s..."

Since he soon had a considerable poke of cash, some unscrupulous people took advantage of Atwell's trust and left with the promise they would quickly pay back what they had borrowed. Martin never got a penny back.

Folks said Martin never made a fuss about being scammed. He moved out of the State House and back to his wigwam, resumed guiding and picked up other odd jobs, and made enough to live on.

Trout fishing and hunting were good in those days. In the summer, Atwell was known to sit out in front of his wigwam and play his fiddle. Some said the tunes were "mournful things in memory of that girl." During the winter, with his wigwam blanketed with sometimes as much as six feet of snow, he also played his fiddle and read every word of each newspaper he could get hold of.

Atwell was superstitious. He had a dried-up weasel nailed over his door to keep witches away. He thought it was bad luck to stick wood through the griddle in the top of the wood stove. He insisted on loading up the stove through the door at the end of the firebox.

Cool claimed Atwell Martin had little ambition. He was skillful enough to survive, but never was what you'd call an expert at hunting, trapping or for that matter acting as a guide. 🍵

The outing party posed, hungrily anticipating the fancied smell of supper the guides would soon prepare. *Courtesy North Elba Historical Society*

CHAPTER 4

Roselle Putney Was a Lumber Camp Cook

REPORTS OF ATWELL MARTIN'S ability to consume enormous quantities of food are persistent, some fanciful. He was also noted for the sincere, yet quaint and humorous, expressions he related to the cook. Those lines would often make an even larger impression than that made by the quantity of food he could pack away.

Lib Brunson told Roselle Putney that she and her husband, Wash, were playing cards one evening when Atwell came by. Lib recalled she had "just taken a batch of bread out of the oven and piled the loaves on the far end of the table opposite of where Atwell sat." She covered the loaves with towels to let them cool. Just before bedtime, Lib noticed Atwell was nibbling a piece of bread crust as he played cards with Wash, but thought nothing of it, supposing he had reached under the cloth and broken off a side crust from a loaf, such as sometimes forms on homemade bread.

When Lib arose in the morning, much to her surprise, she found the men playing seven-up and Atwell still nibbling. Lib noted the cloth she had placed over the bread now lay flat on the table's surface except for a slight rise at one end. Atwell Martin was eating the remains of her last loaf; he had eaten the entire batch of five loaves during the night.

Atwell never confessed to eating the bread, although Lib's husband fessed up to the truth once his visitor had departed.

Roselle Putney remembered Atwell was always polite, thanking her for how she always put up an extra big lunch for him in a pack basket, or when she would offer him a large amount of the soda biscuits she was noted for.

Roselle's gingerbread and suet pudding were among Atwell Martin's favorites. A small amount of fine-tuning to eliminate the butter and lard in Putney's gingerbread recipe follows.

Recipe   **OLD FASHIONED GINGERBREAD**

Roselle Putney's gingerbread made at the lumber camp was a prime dessert her assistant lugged in a big pack basket of goodies to wherever the Perry's logging crew was available for one of their two daily snacks.

½ cup shorting

½ cup sugar

1 egg

½ cup light molasses

1½ cups all-purpose flour

¾ tsp. salt

¾ tsp. soda

½ tsp. ground ginger

½ tsp. ground cinnamon

½ cup boiling water

Directions: Cream shortening and sugar till light. Add egg and molasses; beat thoroughly. Sift together dry ingredients. Add to creamed mixture alternately with water, beating after each addition. Bake in greased and lightly floured 8x8x2-inch pan at 350° for 25 to 40 minutes or till done. Serve warm.

WHEN ROSELLE PUTNEY of Forestport was cooking for Gideon Perry's lumber camp in the Little Woodhull country, Atwell Martin was scaling logs one season. He boarded with the men in a frame house at Reed's Mill.

One morning Roselle made hot soda biscuits for breakfast. As the men were going out to their job, Atwell picked up his pack basket lunch, hefted

1931. The beauty of the Adirondacks seen from the head of North Lake.
Courtesy Roy E. Wires (The Emily Mitchell Wires Collection)

it and said plaintively to Mrs. Putney: "Miss Putney, you ain't got any of them soda biscuits left have you, to put in for chinking?"

Atwell was known to be shy of women. He was never shy when it came to speaking up for food he didn't have to prepare—especially Mrs. Putney's baked goods.

Byron-Curtiss felt the same way about both Mrs. Putney's and Mrs. Brown's cooking. The Reverend said of the noted area cooks that the women's home-made ice cream and pies were a great treat to his daughters. "Helen and Catherine were both good cooks in their own right," he said, "but the meals I took them to at the State House were memorable affairs."

| Recipe | **ROSELLE PUTNEY'S FRESH APPLE BREAD** |

Beat together:

⅓ cup shortening.

1 cup sugar.

Add 1 egg and beat.

Sift together 2 cups of flour, ¾ teaspoons baking powder and ½ teaspoon baking soda and add alternately ⅓ to ½ cup of orange juice.

Stir in 1 cup finely chopped or grated apple, ¼ cup finely chopped walnuts and 1 tablespoon orange rind.

Grease well one 9" x 5" x 3" bread pan. Pour batter into pan. Make indentation with spoon down center. Bake at 350° F. Bake for 1 hour, or until toothpick inserted in center comes out dry and clean. Cool on wire racks for 10 minutes. Carefully remove from pan and continue to cool.

Modern baking tip: *Line the bottom of the pan with parchment paper cut to fit. After cooling for 10 minutes carefully remove bread from pan, peel off paper, and continue cooling.*

The boys prepared supper which was the best ever; then as we ladies, who believe in miracles, took the children fishing, the men washed the dishes. *Author's Collection*

CHAPTER 5

Atwell Martin's Gnawing Hunger

THE TIME was the 1880s. The Beach brothers were all fired up. Ben Beach had recently purchased a new rifle and wanted to go into the Adirondacks to try it out.

Harry arranged for Atwell to guide his three brothers to Horn Lake.

As successful as they had been on their first season with Atwell, it was not without an incident that added to their guide's reputation.

> **Harry Beach:** *While Atwell knew the area well, and was good at carrying a fully-loaded pack, making camp, chopping wood and the like, he was a bit untidy and careless in washing up. So Ben did the cooking for our party. It seemed impossible to fill Old Atwell up. He was always scraping his plate and asking for more.*

The brothers knew from experience that their guide was a glutton—if food was available. He was known to have eaten half a deer when he had it. On the other hand, he was also known to have lived on a single chipmunk for a week.

On this outing the men were watching their bony-framed guide wolf down a stack of pancakes and many strips of bacon, and gulp down cup after cup of coffee, all at breakneck speed. At the end of the meal, and just for fun, they put into action a plan they had hatched earlier.

Harry Beach reports this true account:

"After breakfast, Joe said, 'Atwell, we better have our lunch now. It might be easier and save the bother of stopping to set up our cooking pots at noon if we eat our lunch now.' The old hermit answered: 'Just as ya say, Mr. Beach. Lunch naturally comes after breakfast anyways so why wait. Fetch on the grub.' So we mixed another pail of flapjack batter, fried another pan of salt pork and boiled another pot of coffee and shoved it at him. He ate it all, to our astonishment.

"Just for deviltry, as Atwell was chewing the last pork rind and wiping his tin plate with a slice of bread, I quizzed him. 'Atwell, you might have your supper now? We could then push right through 'til nightfall.' At that suggestion, he didn't even blink when he asserted, 'well, you see it's a matter of course, supper comes after lunch; why wait on them formalities?' Atwell propped himself against the butt of a tree and looked like he was ready and willing to consume more food! If he had any hint of our little plot, he never let on. So the boys set to making another huge batch of flapjacks, another pot of coffee, and frying their last hunk of salt pork. Atwell did that full justice, putting down that feed to the last crumb.

"As he filled his pipe for a smoke, the party washed the soiled dishes and stowed them in the pack. Joe then directed, 'Come on now, Atwell, we are late and we must hit the trail.' But to our surprise he looked up from his comfortable post and calmly informed us he never worked after supper. Our deep plot was not working out right. Giving Atwell the works was like putting the cat in the cage with the canary.

"A contented smile began to move across his face. He belched and beamed on us to show his appreciation of our kindred spirits. Atwell was sitting pretty. All was well with his world. It was obvious he was not about to budge. He forgave us for our misunderstanding the proper succession of his daily routine and began to converse affably about this and that until he locked into a mellow reminiscence.

"Having thus delivered his tales, Atwell proceeded to unroll his blanket and prepare for sleep. We reminded him that we had had all of our meals and were ready for a day of hunting, unhampered by any stops for culinary operations before returning to our boats.

"Atwell was low in tone but quite firm. 'Sleep ALWAYS follows supper. We've et, so now we should lay down to sleep.' Humbly we asked if he

Atwell Martin's hermitage near the foot of North Lake.
Courtesy of the Maitland C. DeSormo Collection

would be ready to start out if we cooked up some breakfast. 'Well, I always like a good breakfast,' he rejoined, 'before I start a day's work. What are we waiting for?'"

| Recipe | **BEN BEACH'S SCRATCH FLAPJACKS** |

1 egg.

1½ cups milk.

2 tablespoons melted lard.

1¼ cups flour.

1 teaspoon sugar.

½ teaspoon baking soda.

½ teaspoon salt.

Blend egg, milk, and lard. Blend dry ingredients. Add to liquids. Fry in skillet with generous amount of lard.

Atwell, New York's post office. *Courtesy Roy E. Wires (The Emily Mitchell Wire's Collection)*

Opposite: Site of Atwell Martin's former hermitage is marked by a pile of stones at the end of an unmarked footpath near the State's sign-in kiosk. *Photograph by William J. O'Hern*

AS NITTY AND I walked along the pathway that led to the site of Atwell's wigwam hermitage, Nit related that someone staying at the State House once asked Atwell how old he was.

His reply was, "Well, I ain't 80 and I ain't 90, but I'm some old, however."

One day Dr. Wiggins was at his camp at North Lake. Someone asked him to take a look at Martin.

Ernestine Koenig puts up the mail in her tiny Atwell Post Office, 1951.
Courtesy Utica Daily Press

Spring Trout & Strawberry Pancakes: Borrowed Tales, Quirky Cures, Camp Recipes

Early spring view from the foot of North Lake. Visitors return to Atwell, New York's remote, hospitable environment in the southwest Adirondacks year after year to enjoy the natural beauty of the wild-feeling land. *Photograph by author*

The doctor was reported to have said, "Boys, you'd better get this old man out of here." Billy Mulchi, who drove the stage for years between Forestport and North Lake, took Atwell to the Herkimer County Home at Middleville.

Martin died there in 1894.

Two years following his death, as I related in "Tall Tales of Atwell Martin,"[4] North Lake's camp owners "succeeded in getting a post office." Since Atwell Martin had been the area's chief landmark for decades, it was only natural to name the tiny post office for him. Byron Cool wanted the building to be named "Martin" but the United States Post Office felt there were too many other "Martins," so they decided on Atwell. The tiny post office remains to this day beside the abandoned State House, the lake's other chief landmark.

Nitty and other North Lakers regret the absence of an official historic marker at the site of Atwell's shanty. The only monument is a cairn of stones at the end of a short trail. Atop the pile has been placed a rusty circular saw blade from an old mill with a faded painted inscription identifying it as the site of the North Lake hermit's home.

CHAPTER 6

We Lived in Nat Foster Lodge

Melancholy incident to record this day! Last evening the largest and best of the trout were reserved for use at the frugal meals to be served on this last day. They were placed in a pail in the spring with proper weights; said weights being some soaked "hard bread rocks." But alas! On His Holiness's going to the spring this morning to get a trout for breakfast, they were gone. An otter or some other varmint of the woods had robbed the deposit of its fishy treasure. Proof that it was not a man, but an animal who committed the theft is evident by the fact that six bottles of Dominican ale in the spring were untouched!

　　　　　　　　　　　　　　—A.L. Byron-Curtiss, July 28, 1905

MY WIFE, BETTE, and I have always loved spending time in the Adirondacks, and for a long time it had been our fondest dream to do so through an entire year. However, all we had for shelter was a backpacking tent—hardly sufficient long-term housing against inclement weather and voracious black flies and mosquitoes.

Our solution was to rent the former Nat Foster Lodge, once owned by Rev. Byron-Curtiss, for one year.

The interior had changed little in the years since the holy man had sold the camp to Tom and Doris Kilbourn in the early 1950s. The only major enhancements Tom had added were gas lights, a propane refrigerator and cook stove, a small shower and a hot water heater.

Living there, mostly on weekends, made for a terrific outdoor life. We had shelter during storms, took canoe trips right from the camp's beach, enjoyed the warmth of a wood fire when we returned in cold weather, enjoyed the sounds and sights of the loon dance in the path of moonlight and felt the presence of the former owner. Nature offers a balm for all ills and a solution for all problems. Life at Nat Foster Lodge was a relaxed and heartening experience.

Food preparation was a snap at Nat Foster Lodge too. We had the conveniences of home within the walls of a rustic camp.

Bette and I enjoyed reading the extensive notes in the camp's log books, and learned that over the decades Byron-Curtiss's camp opening routine had always included leveling the foundation under the front portion of the camp, cleaning the mice nests out of the cook stove, inspecting and cleaning the stove pipes, "slicing up" the camp's interior, sawing down trees into blocks, collecting limbs and driftwood—and replenishing the ever-dwindling woodpile.

Nat Foster Lodge. November 1947. *Courtesy Jeb Brees*

1947. St. Catherine's Outdoor Chapel, Nat Foster Lodge, North Lake. *Courtesy Jeb Brees*

Wooden boat repairs were many. They needed to be moved from storage and repaired. Just moving the weighty boats down a makeshift ramp and into the water was more than a one-man job.

Docks, of course, needed yearly attention, and other carpentry projects big and small never seemed to diminish. The weight of winter's snow on his structure and the action of frost on the "upright," constructed from salvaged lumber that was not always the best to begin with, ensured yearly rebuilding and repairing.

The addition of the fireplace in 1930 was the last major remodeling job the owner undertook.

And, there were the myriad tiny details a non-camp owner might never give a thought to: "Put new oar locks on boat. Built a saw horse. Put yellow trim on big boat and proper lettering on Omega." There were also the necessary but mundane jobs of washing clothing with scrub board and tub, washing windows, daily cleaning of the kerosene lamp globes and trimming wicks, putting up muslin screens over the windows, and tending to sewing and mending tasks.

Those jobs were not part of our experience at Nat Foster. We enjoyed the leisure to just recreate and use the facilities. About the only chore, if it could be called that, was to bring drinking water from a trusted spring, a mile away on the opposite shore. The job was easy, filling large water containers and then driving them to the camp. It reminded Bette of her childhood days when she and her siblings had carried drinking water in gallon glass jugs from her aunt's house to hers. Their house had no well and lacked indoor plumbing. Nat Foster didn't have potable water, but it did have flush toilets that used lake water.

Rev. Byron-Curtiss, who other North Lake campers dubbed the "Bishop of North Lake," gave new meaning to the old saying, "A woman's work is never done" through the many notations in his log books of all the work he accomplished around his camp. Food preparation was time-consuming. Whether baking bread or making a pot of beans, cooking was always performed on a wood-fired cook stove—not a simple task when even temperatures are required for best results, which required constant tending to the cast-iron woodstove.

Bette and I didn't make meals that required a lot of preparation. We did, however, have mouth-watering mealtimes. Chicken recipes are always tasty and easy to prepare. "Panther Spring Chicken, Sausage & Potatoes" and "Nat Foster's Italian Style Stew" are favorite recipes that included meat.

Recipe | **PANTHER SPRING CHICKEN, SAUSAGE & POTATOES**

Ingredients:

2–3 lbs. cut-up chicken.

1 lb. hot or sweet Italian sausage.

1 cup red dry or semi-dry wine.

1 cup water.

5 lbs. wedged potatoes (We like red).

¼ teaspoon salt.

¼ teaspoon pepper.

⅛ teaspoon garlic powder.

½ teaspoon oregano.

garnish finished dish with fresh parsley.

Directions: Combine chicken, cut-up sausage, onion and potatoes in large roasting pan. Sprinkle with all of the spices. Mix wine and water and pour all over ingredients. Cover and bake at 375°F. for 1½ hours. Serve.

Recipe NAT FOSTER'S ITALIAN STYLE STEW

Ingredients:
3 ½ to 4 lbs. chicken, cut up.
2 medium onions.
½ teaspoon pepper.
2 cups diced potatoes.
1 teaspoon oregano.
½ cup water.
2 teaspoons salt.
1 stalk celery, sliced.
8 oz. tomatoes.
3 tablespoons parsley.
1 cup fresh or frozen peas.
Directions: Brown chicken and add onions. Sauté 5 minutes. Arrange celery and potatoes in bottom of crock pot. Add chicken, onions, salt, pepper, tomatoes, oregano and parsley. Pour in water. Cover. Cook low 6 to 8 hours. Add peas; cover; cook on high 15 minutes. cook on high 15 minutes.

MOUNTAIN LIVING meant a longer season of cold, too. A chunk of ice needed for the small icebox was purchased from the State House's ice house every few days.

We found vacationing in the old camp nostalgic, and while our tasks there were easier and our life more comfortable than Rev. Byron-Curtiss' had been, it was not at all difficult to imagine ourselves there decades earlier. Even with our minor deprivations, it was clear that the "the good old days" had nothing to recommend them when it came to maintaining a comfortable domicile. Advantages like central heating, vacuum cleaners, electric washing machines, television, the Internet, power tools and other labor-saving devices have made life far better. Turning on a water faucet, adjusting the room thermometer, jumping into a hot shower, wash and wear clothing and all the other time-saving devices that help make a domicile spic-and-span were missing in his day.

We found it interesting to learn that Rev. Byron-Curtiss and some of his camp neighbors responded as many spirit-consuming Americans did during the Prohibition years in America: They began brewing their own beer. Among some "Simple Supper" recipes on a dog-eared scrap of paper is a handwritten recipe titled "My Process for Making 10 to 12 Gallons of Lager Beer." On it he noted some fine tuning: "…once the hops have steeped, place sack in a pan and use a potato masher to squeeze." And, before adding the solution, "…warm the crock with HOT water so as not to chill the compound in the kettle on the woodstove." A curious method for taking the

Mike and Dianne O'Hern. April, 1998. Soon after this picture was taken, the author and his son Mike took the canoe out on the lake. Mike accidently tipped the canoe over, spilling the paddlers into the cold water. Soup and Nat Foster Lodge's box stove warmed the campers up. *Author's Collection*

temperature of the concoction reminds the brewer to bring the temperature of the compound in the crock up to the point that one can "plunge one's hand and forearm in and hold it in the brew aggregation for one minute."

For obvious reasons, there is little specific mention of home brew in the camp logs during Prohibition, but Rev. Byron-Curtiss's skill as a brewer and his willingness to share appear to have further ingratiated him with his friends and neighbors. His fondness for "liquid bait," his words, was quite acceptable among his friends. "Who didn't drink up there in Forestport in those days?" John Todd exclaimed when remembering Byron-Curtiss. "My father, Scudder, called him 'the drinkin' preacher,' and he meant it with the greatest of fondness toward The Reverend."

"Bette and I didn't need a classier veranda to eat under in order to enjoy the tree-cooled setting that seemed to turn wild across the lake." —Jay O'Hern. *Author's Collection*

Another fellow who remembered the preacher as well as his homemade desserts that included rhubarb pie and "Camp Mouse Sugar Cookies" was Robert Buell. His parents owned a camp on the opposite shore. Bob often visited Nat Foster Lodge as a boy and shared the preacher's interesting cookie recipe and this recollection that might indicate that B-C had a sizable stash of "liquid bait":

Recipe **CAMP MOUSE SUGAR COOKIES**

Ingredients:
1 egg.
½ cup shortening, melted.
1 cup sugar.
½ teaspoon cinnamon.
2 tablespoons milk.
1 teaspoon lemon juice.
2 cups sifted all-purpose flour.
1 teaspoon baking powder.
Directions: 1). Preheat the oven to 400°F. 2). Break the egg into a large mixing bowl. Add shortening, sugar, cinnamon, milk and lemon juice. Beat with an egg beater until creamy. 3). Sift the flour and baking powder together into another bowl. Add this mixture into the first bowl and mix well with a spoon. 4). Drop the dough by teaspoonful onto a cookie sheet. (You don't have to grease it.) Leave at least one inch of space between the cookies. 5). Bake for 8 to 10 minutes or until cookies are golden brown. Immediately remove the cookies from the cookie sheet. Place them on a wire rack to cool.

★ ★ ★

BOB SAID this was one of the first cookie recipes he cooked on his own. "It's a good recipe for a child to try," he said.

"I was five years old in 1921, when I first remember B-C coming to my parents' year-round camp in Atwell for a haircut," reminisced Bob, who often referred to Rev. Byron-Curtiss as "B-C."

"Mother cut the parson's hair just the way he liked it. B-C's camp was about a mile and a half up the lake beyond ours. My parents took us kids by boat to attend Sunday church service at his outdoor chapel. He was real friendly to us kids. When we got older we'd take our flat-bottomed rowboats to Nat Foster Lodge to talk to him. He'd always offer us something to eat—usually homemade donuts or cookies. I also remember a jelly roll, because I asked Mother if she'd make his recipe for us."

Recipe   NAT FOSTER LODGE'S JELLY ROLL

Bob Buell dug out B-C's jelly roll from his mother recipe file.
It did not contain a list of ingredients.
Directions:
Beat 4 egg yolks; add gradually ¼ cup sugar, 1 tsp. vanilla.
Beat 4 egg whites almost stiff. Add gradually ½ cup sugar & beat very stiff.
Fold yolks into whites. Then fold in dry ingredients (1 tsp. baking powder, ¼ tsp. salt, ¾ cup sifted flour—take out 1 tbs. flour & add 1 tbs. of corn starch or use ¾ cup sifted cake flour & omit the corn starch).
Spread in wax paper-lined pan about 10½ inches by 10 inches. Bake in 375°F. oven for 12 minutes. Loosen edges of cake & turn out onto towel dusted with confectioner's sugar. Quickly peel off and lay fresh piece of waxed paper on top of cake. Roll quickly & wrap in the towel. When cool, unwrap, unroll, remove paper, spread with filling and roll again.

BOB WAS ENTHUSIASTIC when he talked about B-C. As he examined some sepia-toned snapshots that I had collected on the history of the lake's camps, his facial expressions ran from astonished recognition to outright infectious laughter. The aged photos brought back memories of his family's Atwell camp and fond past times.

"Have I ever got a story for you," he said. "It's about B-C's keen wit. I always get a chuckle when I think of my embarrassment. I was sitting in a wooden chair in Nat Foster Lodge, trying to balance on the back two legs, when I lost my balance and tipped back, banging against the partition wall. I'll never forget it. There was a huge rattling of glass against glass. That was in the days of Prohibition, and I'd heard from Dad that it was thought that Curtiss kept a rather substantial stock of booze squirreled away. So when I heard the clatter I got a little worried. B-C just laughed: 'Don't ye be a-worrying, Bobbie. Those are just my medicine bottles and the former missus' old fruit jars a-rattling around in there.'

"I never saw him inebriated, but I'd heard the cleric liked his drink. I clearly recall watching him canoe from camp to camp in the wee hours of the morning when mist was still coming off the water's surface. He always looked like he was glowing as he looked into the food pots and helped himself to a little here and there."

Bob Buell made Nat Foster Lodge a frequent destination. *Author's Collection*

Warnings about the Wandover Clan and the Lopsided Ridge Runner always worked to make Bobbie Buell finish all the food on his plate and to go to sleep when he was told. *Pen and ink drawing by Michael E. O'Hern*

Bob and I worked at the same place. He was head of maintenance in the Camden Central School district; I was a teacher in the middle school. Over time, I believe Bob realized I was quite skilled at finding my way around the deep woods of his youth. The fact that I uncovered several locations of former camps he'd talked about and even managed to uncover pictures of them stunned him.

"The Reverend was very friendly; he was also quite a talker," said Bob. "He'd tell us about an Adirondack foothills 'community camp' he and old George Wandover had hidden in the green timber near Gooseneck Creek. I figured it was in the vicinity of the old Brooks Lumber Camp and dam. It was the most likely spot since the old buildings were ripe for scavenging building materials. There's enough iron tossed around the camp site— and so few spruce have yet replanted themselves—that you can still find the Brooks Camp clearing just above where Gooseneck Creek outlet joins the north branch of the Black River.

"The Wandovers were a local clan with a reputation," Bob witnessed. "City folk found George, the patriarch, to be a gentleman, but Dad said some North Lakers referred to George and his kin as 'stand-ins for the devil.'

"They knew the country like the backs of their hands. George was a well-respected guide. He was also legendary when it came to taking care of his deer-hunting parties. He'd travel far into Township 5, Adirondack League Club territory, just to satisfy his clients' quest for venison. The Wandovers were dyed-in-the-wool game violators. Outlaws, some said, but never to their faces. All I know for sure is that B-C's stories about the Wandovers used to scare the bejesus out of us kids. Mother would only need to mention their name to get us to finish our supper or go to bed, because we were certain one of the Wandovers might come to get us.

"Her tactic was as effective as when she promised us a batch of 'Marshmallow Treats' once we worked up a generous supply of stove wood for the kitchen range."

Bob continued his recollections: "B-C sure was a storyteller. He had bear and deer skulls nailed to his exterior walls. He'd point to a rather large bear skull and tell us kids, 'You see the teeth there? They used to belong to old Paul Bunyan's ox.'

"Of course he warned us to always keep a sharp lookout for the Lopsided Ridge Runner, a half-man, half-animal that was supposed to wander in one direction around the summit of Ice Cave Mountain. The creature was supposed to emerge from the deep, ice-filled crevice on the western edge of

Old 'Red' Louie, Camp 7 cook. *Courtesy Lawton Williams*

the mountaintop about bedtime. He related that Old 'Red' Louie, a cook at Camp 7, Gould's Ice Cave Mountain lumber camp, once swore he detected strange sounds coming down off the mountain. The Frenchy became more than curious and climbed the mountain to investigate. As he rounded the ridge he spied a long, gangly creature with one leg shorter than the other. It could only run clockwise because its right leg was shorter than the left, similar to how the legs of a lookout platform would appear if built out over a ledge. Red's eyesight wasn't all that good, but he thought he might even have seen what appeared to be a small child kicking and screaming but unable to escape the lock-arm grip of the Lopsided Ridge Runner.

"B-C made other claims, too. One in particular was in connection with one of the few technological improvements, the sawmill he had at camp. He didn't care for too many modern machine-age improvements. I think his philosophy had more to do with the fact that he lived on a limited income. I heard him more than once sermonize how man in large measure should pattern himself after nature. That is to say, man should be more or less free, flexible, and not exactly rigged like a precise piece of machinery. He'd pick up a leaf in the bright sun and examine it, the veins and threads of division radiating from the center. Then he'd point out that each leaf, while unique, did follow a general pattern. 'See here Bobbie,' he'd say, 'Man, like the leaf, should be free, yet orderly.' I guess I thought of him as some sort of a scientist or philosopher but never put a label to it.

"I well remember he would point to his sawmill and say, 'You see there, I wrote about that accomplishment.'" Bob's recall was spot-on. I found Rev. Byron-Curtiss did record his achievement in the May 1917 camp journal entry in large letters.

The journal tells that Rev. Byron-Curtiss' novel piece of machinery arrived at the Forestport Station train depot. After a cold ride from the lake on a bleak early May day to pick it up, he set to work installing it. He rigged up the attachment that made his sawmill possible; the power came from an Evinrude outboard motor, which he fastened to a plank spiked between

Joseph Byron-Curtiss sharpening his father's outboard sawmill blade. "Nat Foster Lodge was not sealed or insulated well. B-C burned a god awful lot of wood."
—Harold NcNitt. *Courtesy Thomas and Doris Kilbourn (The A. L. Byron-Curtiss Collection)*

two trees. He recorded: "It looked most successful when I first put it all together." Bob thought the motor, attachment, and circular saw blade looked like a cobbled affair and yet it was capable of bucking as much limb wood in a few hours as a man could cut by hand in a week.

Here's another thing about B-C that Bob recalled. "He made this claim regarding the North Lake beavers, who upon seeing his gas-driven mill became jealous, wishing they too could become mechanized. 'Why, they were just astonished with my operation, Bobbie. In fact, they thought it was such a good thing that they should have something similar for cutting the trees to obtain limbs for their dams and lodges, since it would save them significant time. One of the beavers, being more intelligent than the others, snuck up to study my setup at night. Lucky for me I was awakened by rustling outside. Sneaking to the open screened window, I spied several beaver talking. The biggest was saying that he had been studying me and had gotten the machine operation down in principle so he could run it as well as any

Byron-Curtiss rescued Bob in his rowboat, the *Cobweb*. *Courtesy Thomas and Doris Kilbourn (The A. L. Byron-Curtiss Collection)*

Lt. to Rt. Unidentified Red Camp guest and Byron Curtiss. "B-C was a very likable person. You just liked being around him as a kid. I just liked him. He had lots of stories. I went over to his camp quite often. We talked a lot about fishing." —Harold McNitt. *Courtesy Harold McNitt*

preacher. They were fixing to plot against me just like when we North Lakers get 'invited' onto Adirondack League Club property. They planned to sell the machinery that night, hauling it clear up to the Mud Hole at the headwaters of the North Branch. I sent 'em packing! They never did come back, probably on account of all the steel traps I placed around the lodge."

"Of course us kids gobbled those things right up.

"One day two friends and I rowed to Cranberry Island. It was a small patch of land a good hundred yards offshore of Nat Foster Lodge, a real nice place to swim, because there was sand all the way around it. I don't know what brought it on, but I got into an argument with my buddy and to get even he rowed away in the boat, leaving my friend and me to fend for ourselves. We were skinny-dipping. I volunteered to save ourselves from our marooned situation when we realized our buddy was not going to return. Carefully, I bundled all my clothing in a compact wad. Placing it on the top of my head, I looped my leather belt over the top. To hold the clothing securely in place I drew in the belt and cinched the load to my

Nat Foster Lodge's fireplace was a focal point where Bob and the Reverend sat and talked. *Courtesy Thomas and Doris Kilbourn (The A. L. Byron-Curtiss Collection)*

head, fastening the belt into the tightest belt hole. The idea worked very well. I had little difficulty swimming to shore. I even arrived with fairly dry clothing. I didn't know it, but B-C had been watching from his camp window. He met me as I emerged from the water stark naked! 'That was a pretty good trick, Bobbie,' he said. His face sparkled with laughter as he offered to loan me his little rowboat so I could return to the island to pick up my friend.

"I was about sixteen when that happened—just the age when I didn't want a tale like that to get out of the bag. You can imagine my surprise and embarrassment when I read about the rescue in the *Boonville Herald* the following week. The Reverend was a regular columnist and wrote a rather flowery story of the experience."

Many things have changed at North Lake since Byron-Curtiss's days there, and yet many others have not. The trout fishing is not what it used to be, and the Adirondack League Club gamekeeper near the head of the lake is a part of history with the Department of Environmental Conservation easement having opened the area. Still, it remains a place to view beautiful scenery and for prayerful reflection on life and God and nature, just as Byron-Curtiss would have it. Current North Lakers hope to keep it that way.

As different as Bette's and my lives and the times are from Rev. Byron-Curtiss's, we were equally awed and inspired by the headwaters of the Black River region of the Adirondacks. We have also kept one large glass Mason jar he used for storing nuts as a memory piece of our days at the camp. I like to think it might have been one of those suspicious bottles Bob Buell talked about. We have also baked his famous jelly roll and rhubarb pie, and from time to time have made Bob's mother's Marshmallow Treats.

I have assumed Rev. Byron-Curtiss and the head cook of Gould Paper Company's Lumber Camp 10 shared recipes. The log books tell he spent time at the nearby lumber camp. His rhubarb pie recipe is identical to the one that appears in Emily Mitchell Wires' Camp Cozy cookbook. Her camp was a short distance from Nat Foster Lodge

Recipe CAMP 10 RHUBARB PIE

Ingredients: 2 cups rhubarb.

1½ cups sugar mixed with one rounded tablespoon flour.

Butter the size of a walnut—melted.

1 egg.

Directions: Mix sugar, flour, pinch of salt; add beaten egg, melted butter. Pour over rhubarb and mix well. Bake in pastry—top crust can be latticed. Oven 450°F. for ten minutes—reduce to 350°F. and bake until juice has boiled up thru slits in crust. Then bake 5 min. longer.

Recipe | **MOTHER BUELL'S MARSHMALLOW TREATS**

Ingredients:

¼ cup of butter or margarine.

½ teaspoon cinnamon.

40 regular or 4 cups of miniature marshmallows.

5 cups Rice Krispies® cereal.

1 cup coconut.

½ cup walnuts.

Directions: Melt butter or margarine in large saucepan over low heat. Add marshmallows and stir until completely melted. Cook over low heat 3 minutes longer, stirring constantly. Remove from heat. Stir in ½ teaspoon cinnamon. Add Rice Krispies®, coconut and walnuts. Stir until well coated. Using waxed paper, press mixture into buttered 13x9x2 inch pan. Cut into two-inch squares when cool.

CHRONIC ARTHRITIC PAIN, a bitter divorce, the deaths of two of his children and the intermittent, paralyzing depression he referred to as his "nervous disorder" created a new kind of wilderness with which Rev. Byron-Curtiss had no experience, and one his friends could not effectively guide him through. They offered what comfort they could, and that often included enjoying a shared meal.

Charley and Anna Brown lived at the State House. Anna Brown's cooking added a nice touch to camp life and reminded Rev. Byron-Curtiss of being close to his daughters when they had all been at camp together.

Mrs. Brown made the preacher many pies that first year of his retirement, and visiting friends and relatives supplied other food and material comforts.

B-C was also a frequent guest at the Browns' dinner table. A meal with the Browns brought friends together.

AN ANNA BROWN STATE HOUSE DINNER MENU: Bread & butter, pickles, Irish stew, Escalloped onions, spinach, pork & beans and trout.coffee, jam & crackers

Recipe | **FORESTPORT ESCALLOPED ONIONS**

Pare and slice enough onions to fill a baking dish; parboil in water till tender. Butter dish and put in a layer of onions, sprinkle over a layer of crumbs, and add salt and pepper and a few bits of butter. Then place another layer of onions, etc. until the dish is full. Have the last layer crumbs. Put bits of butter over the top; then pour ½ cup of cream overall and bake in a moderate oven one hour or less according to the size of the dish. 🍵

Bette O'Hern, Black River flume. The destination along the North Lake road is a popular short path to the picnic-swimming-fishing site. McMartin's *Discover the Southwestern Adirondacks* guidebook describes the route. *Photograph by author*

A Background of Foothills, Forest, and Mountains

SPRING TROUT AND STRAWBERRY PANCAKES is a story of a vanished lifestyle, but also a story of an Adirondack land and some of its earlier inhabitants. The land has not lost its beauty, its charm, and its appeal. The roadways reaching into the North Country have changed, the camps spoken about have new owners and in some cases are gone, the once well-known and interesting people who were camp owners have passed on, and some of the former private land is now state-owned.

But, the years have been good to the mountains and forest. Unbridled logging has stopped, waterways are protected, large chunks of state land have been parceled into primitive, wild forest, and wilderness designations—decrees that are not always popular. Owners of camps and cottages settled in the Adirondacks for a variety of reasons. Peaceful living was a motivation for some but not all mountain people were summer visitors. Atwell Martin, the Browns, the Putneys, and Getmans called the country "home." They worked in the lumber woods, managed boarding houses, dealt with deep plunges in temperature and blizzards but were as charmed by the year-round beauty and peace of the Adirondacks as their summer visitors.

This land of contentment can be revisited through pictures, recipes, and remembrances. The lakes are still there, the forested mountains still stand; the air is still crisp and the sky as blue as on a day a hundred years ago; some early buildings remain but now are furnished with electricity and "new-fangled" kitchen machines that make preparing food much easier than in the past.

The stories here are told through the lives of those I have listened to and known—men and women working, talking, relaxing, and eating. As they come and go, time moves backward and forward with them. That too is the way all that we remember comes and goes. ❦

If you ever dream about the good old times, just be reminded of the lack of modern labor-saving household equipment that now helps keep our homes clean and families fed without breaking backs. *Public Domain*

CHAPTER 7

Opening Camp

SPRING CAMP OPENING is filled with variables. It's dependent on the location, the owner, whether the owner has a hired caretaker, and the weather. I have on their opening day helped several Adirondack cottage owners who used to share their camp with me. The routine was a comfortable one. Absolutely necessary jobs were performed quickly, like turning on the water system, repairs to the outhouse, fixing tears in window screening, picking up branches and twigs, and inspecting the roof, chimneys, and stove pipes.

I've never opened a camp without seeing a reminder that no matter how diligently one tries, it is impossible to declare the building 100% mouse-proof. As a result, a thorough cleaning of their "calling cards" is also necessary. Other tasks such as boat and dock repairs, getting boats into the water, starting outboard motors that have been idle all winter, and other chores are eventually gotten to, but at a slower pace. Some work often stretched over an entire month of May weekends.

What I remember most about opening camp day with my grandparents, beyond the excitement of just returning to the place, was the difference between what my grandfather fixed to eat and the real meals Grandma prepared when she was in camp.

Grandpa always warmed up a can of Franco-American® spaghetti and buttered up slices of white bread, sometimes sprinkled with sugar, that we'd eat along with what fish we had caught. When Grandma was along, there would be no canned food.

My grandparents completed necessary work at Camp Oasis but without the stress of absolute deadlines. Fishing, tarrying, and putting more emphasis on getting out on the water came right after the necessary weekend work. They made it feel like a vacation agenda. How I looked forward to our first freshly-caught fish of the year and my grandmother's Honey Dipped Donuts, Cinnamon Twist and Cherry Walnut Coffeecake, Fanned Fig Cake, and her yeast dough Prune Kuchen. The homey aroma of great-tasting yeast bread baking in the kitchen oven was my signal to rise from the unheated attic bedroom and come downstairs.

The Camp Oasis cookbook contains some conventional yeast recipes. My favorite Prune Kuchen is not among them, unfortunately. I believe Grandma was an intuitive cook. She didn't always need a recipe to follow. There is a large section my grandmother's recipe book labeled "Fish, Game & Chicken." The eighty-one recipes all revolved around her garden produce, fish that we caught, chicken which we raised and game my grandfather secured. I'll venture the majority of modern cookbooks don't have a section like that because people obtain their food differently and choose to eat differently.

Camp Oasis. Author's grandparents' camp. *Author's Collection*

Five camp meals I remember helping to prepare and enjoyed eating were easy to make, and I find them as current today as they were a generation ago. Grandma's Fanned Fig Cake is a conventional yeast recipe. It takes time to prepare. You might like to try it the way she did when she made that great-tasting bread with the warm, homey aroma I can still remember.

Recipe   **BAKED FISH WITH CORN FLAKES**

Use any favorite filet of fish. Dip in canned milk, then in corn flake crumbs, and bake in 300°F. oven until golden brown. Salt and pepper to taste.

Recipe   **MARINATED CARROT AND BEAN SALAD**

Ingredients:

8 medium carrots, peeled and cut into 2-inch julienne strips.

½ teaspoon sugar.

1 pound tender young green beans.

Albert Zysset, author's grandfather relaxing at camp. *Author's Collection*

Author's grandmother, Ethel Zysset is third from left, seated with a group at her Food Lovers Summer Party at Camp Oasis. *Author's Collection*

2 tablespoons chopped fresh tarragon.

2 tablespoons chopped fresh parsley.

¼ cup dry white wine.

¾ cup light olive oil.

2 tablespoons white wine vinegar.

2 tablespoons lemon juice.

¼ cup toasted slivered almonds (optional).

Lettuce leaf cups.

Directions: Place carrots in heavy saucepan with one inch boiling water. Add sugar and dash salt and pepper. Cover, reduce heat and simmer until carrots are tender-crisp, about 5 to 7 minutes. Drain* and set aside. Remove tips and strings from beans and cut in 2-inch pieces. Cook in small amount of boiling salted water just until tender-crisp, about 10 minutes. Blanch quickly in cold water to stop the cooking process. Drain well and set aside. Combine tarragon, parsley, onions, garlic, wine, oil, vinegar and lemon juice in small bowl, mixing well. Pour half of dressing over carrots and half over green beans in separate bowls. Cover vegetables and chill well. To serve, toss vegetables together and season to taste with salt and pepper. Spoon into crisp lettuce leaf cups. Sprinkle with slivered almonds. Makes 6 to 8 servings.

Cooking juice was saved and used for soup broth.

Recipe **ACORN SQUASH RINGS AND GREEN BEANS**

Ingredients:

2 acorn squash, trimmed.

4 tablespoons butter.

1½ pounds green beans, trimmed.

1 tablespoon Worcestershire sauce.

¼ teaspoon pepper.

Directions: 1). Preheat oven to 350°F. 2). Bake squash in pre-heated oven for 30 minutes. Remove squash from oven; leave oven on. Slice each squash into 3 equal rings, about 1 inch thick. Compost seeds and pulp. 3). Melt 1 tablespoon of the butter in small saucepan. Brush squash slices with butter. Arrange in 13x9x2-inch baking dish. 4). Return to oven and bake 30 to 35 minutes or until tender. 5). Meanwhile, cook green beans in boiling salted water to cover in large saucepan, 5 to 10 minutes or until crisp-tender. 6). Melt remaining 3 table-spoons butter in same small saucepan. Stir in Worcestershire sauce and pepper. Divide beans into 6 equal bunches and stuff one bunch into center of each squash ring.

Gram noted that the squash rings with beans would be arranged "around the holiday duck, turkey, pork roast or braised tongue."

Recipe **QUICK HOMEMADE SLOPPY JOES**

Ingredients:

1 lb. ground beef.

¼ cup chopped onion.

¼ cup chopped green peppers.

¼ cup chopped celery.

1 cup (8 oz.) tomato sauce.

1 tablespoon vinegar.

1 tablespoon sugar.

1½ teaspoons Worcestershire sauce.

1 teaspoon salt.

⅛ teaspoon pepper.

Directions: Brown meat, add vegetables, sauce and seasonings and simmer 20 minutes.

Gram served these on home-baked yeast rolls.

July 1947. The author's water adventures began when he was 2 years 8 months.
Author's Collection

FANNED FIG CAKE

Ingredients:

½ cup milk.

½ cup sugar.

1½ teaspoons salt.

¼ cup (½ stick) butter or margarine.

½ cup warm water (105°F.–115°F.).

2 packages active dry yeast.

2 eggs, beaten.

4½ to 5½ cups unsifted flour.

1 egg yolk.

2 tablespoons milk.

Gram with author, July 1946

Directions: Scald ½ cup milk; stir in sugar, salt, and butter or margarine. Cool to lukewarm. Measure warm water into large warm bowl. Sprinkle in yeast; stir until dissolved. Add lukewarm milk mixture, eggs and 3 cups flour. Beat until smooth. Stir in enough additional flour to make a stiff dough. Turn out onto lightly floured board; knead until smooth and elastic, about 8 to 10 minutes. Place in greased bowl, turning to grease top. Cover; let rise in warm place, free from draft, until doubled in bulk, about 1 hour.

Meanwhile, while the dough rises, prepare the Fig Filling and Crumb Topping.

Fig Filling: In a saucepan combine 1 cup chopped dried figs, ¼ cup firmly packed brown sugar, ⅔ cup water, and 1 tablespoon lemon juice. Bring to a boil over medium heat, stirring. Continue cooking until mixture is thick enough to spread. Remove from heat; stir in ½ cup chopped pecans.

Crumb Topping: In a small bowl combine ¼ cup unsifted flour, 2 tablespoons sugar and ½ teaspoon ground cinnamon. Using a pastry cutter or 2 knives, cut in 2 tablespoons of margarine or butter until mixture resembles coarse meal.

Punch dough down once it has doubled; turn out onto lightly floured board. Divide dough in half. Roll each half into an oblong, 9x18 inches. Spread ½ of prepared filling on ⅔ of length of dough. Fold unspread dough over ½ of spread dough. Then fold again, making 3 layers of dough and 2 layers of filling. Seal edges. Place on greased baking sheets. Using scissors, cut 8 strips, along length of rectangle to within 1 inch of opposite side. Separate strips slightly and twist so that filling shows. Cover; let rise in warm place, free from draft, until doubled in bulk, about 1 hour.

Brush cakes with egg yolk beaten with 2 tablespoons milk. Sprinkle with prepared topping. Bake at 350°F. about 20 minutes, or until done. Remove from baking sheets and cool on wire racks. Makes 2 coffee cakes.

The author's overnight water junkets have continued for decades. The warning protestations of child-rearing loon, lily pads in shallow water, turtles, frogs and fish in deeper water are part of the Adirondack adventure. *Author's Collection*

CHAPTER 8

Vintage Cookbooks

Spring means new awakenings
In flower, bird, and bee,
But none is a greater miracle
Than the sap in the maple tree.

—unknown poet

ANNA BROWN'S COOKBOOK was typical of the many cookbooks of the day. All were filled with family recipes, dog-eared pages of recipes that must have been darlings and included notations such as, "The following dish was passed down to me by my grandmother of her old days...," unusual-today dishes, and meals that stretched meat and the dollar but still offered nutritious table fare.

Anna's cookery was typical too in that the section written in longhand offered complete "lunches, supper or lunch and supper menus," like the one noted in the previous chapter. All included homemade breads of some kind or other.

Maple syrup is still one of New York's sweetest harvests. Anna's memory of a hearty long-ago invitation to "Come on over tonight—we're a-goin' to sugar off" surely was a fond one, as were the many recipes she listed: Maple Baked Beans, Maple Sugar Biscuits, Maple Drop Cookies, Maple Ice Cream, and Maple Butternut Fudge.

Recipe **MAPLE SUGAR BISCUITS**

Make a very rich, tender baking powder biscuit crust, using milk instead of water. Roll out about half the thickness of ordinary biscuit and cut into shapes with the cover of a quarter-pound baking powder can or caddy. As every other biscuit is cut, sprinkle bits of maple sugar on top, moisten the next biscuit and press down on top of the sugared one. Lay close together in baking pan so that they will rise instead of spreading. Brush over with milk or melted butter and bake in quick oven till brown. Serve at once with saucers of warm maple syrup.

1896. Anna Brown's State House dining room. The table setting is covered to keep flies off. *Courtesy Thomas and Doris Kilbourn (The A. L. Byron-Curtiss Collection)*

MAPLE BUTTERNUT FUDGE

2 cups of maple sugar.

½ cup of cream.

Boil until it strings from the spoon; then add 1 cup of chopped butternuts and pour to cool in a buttered pan.

DEPENDING ON THE TREES from which the sap is collected and the method used to boil it down, syrups have subtle flavor variations, classified commercially as grades. Nevertheless, anyone who has grown up with real maple syrup—not maple-flavored corn syrup—can instantly tell the difference. Mary Lovejoy Thomas's first recollection of maple syrup is a sweet one indeed:

Christmas in the 1950s did not mean that my brother and I would find a pile of toys under the tree. I remember one year when my brother

Sap making in the Adirondacks. *Courtesy Town of Webb Historical Association*

got a slightly-used bicycle and took steel wool to the rust, hoping he could pass it off as new to his friends. The same year, I got a doll that drank and wet, but did not "shed real tears" like the Tiny Tears doll I'd wanted, so I was little disappointed.

One thing in which we were never disappointed was the package that arrived from our Aunt Esther, who lived in Vermont. She was the food columnist for their little local newspaper, and had a maple syrup side-line. I don't know how much syrup the sugar bush produced, but we always knew that our aunt's Christmas package would contain a big bottle of it. It had a vaguely smoky taste, maybe because it was cooked in a vat outside over an open fire. It was heaven on homemade waffles or pancakes, but what we were really looking for as we pawed through the wads of newspaper in the package was a heavy round tin of what Mother referred to as "Aunt Esther's Perfect Fudge." This was a great treat for children who were rarely allowed to eat candy or drink soda pop.

The delicious concoction would make its appearance again when Mother took us to visit our aunt's camp in the summer. The "no sugar" rules were relaxed for the time we were on vacation. At least once during the visit, Aunt Esther would wink at Mother and say, "I don't feel much like making supper. Do you think the kids would mind if we just had popcorn and fudge tonight?" Auntie had no children of her own, and she loved to spoil us. Mother would give in without much reluctance, with the caveat that milk and apples would also be included.

It's still a favorite camp supper, one that makes even an old lady feel positively devious!

Recipe   **AUNT ESTHER'S PERFECT MAPLE FUDGE**

Ingredients:

1½ cup pure maple syrup (not maple-flavored).

1¾ cup sugar.

Small can (5 ounce) evaporated milk.

¼ teaspoon salt.

½ stick butter (4 tablespoons).

1 teaspoon vanilla.

1 cup chopped walnuts (black walnuts if you like them).

Directions: Butter an 8" square pan. Combine syrup, sugar, milk and salt in a medium saucepan. Stirring constantly, bring to a boil over medium-high heat. Once it is boiling, cook without stirring until it registers 238° F. Remove the pan from the heat. Beat in the butter and vanilla. Let the mixture cool slightly. Then beat like crazy until it is thick, lighter in color and loses its gloss. Stir in the walnuts and spread into prepared pan. Try to wait about half an hour before you cut it into squares. 🐟

Mom's 1930s cookbook shows the scars of use, incurred when she switched to a new and unfamiliar electric cooking range. *Photograph by author*

CHAPTER 9

Gram's Jack Wax Party

TO EVERY BOY growing up in the icy foothills of the Adirondacks, early spring signaled the annual maple sugar harvest and jack wax parties. Silas Conrad Kimm was no exception. Silas lived and worked in Salisbury, N.Y. When Silas was eleven years of age, he hired out to do farm work; chores included milking, mowing fields of hay, sawing, splitting, piling wood and most likely working in the sugar bush. All work was done by hand in those days. Farms in northern Herkimer Country in the years following the Civil War did not have the kind of farm machinery that would later come to improve the lot of the hard-working farmer.

Not the least of assets from the nearby woods were maple products. Early spring marked a time of freezing nights and welcome sunny days. That combination meant sap would be running in the hard maples.

Tapping trees while some snow still lay on the ground, collecting sap buckets, and making maple syrup and sugar was almost a night-and-day task on those old farms. The entire operation involved a lot of work but it was not without its fun, at least in reflection.

"Sugarbushes" were located at the edges of the farms. The sugar shanty was where the boys and men would lie, often on buffalo robes, late into the night waiting for the sap to boil, watching not to let the pan run dry or the syrup run over. There, Silas would listen to the stories the men told, drop some whole eggs into the boiling sap whenever they got hungry, and wait for the time when he could pour some of the syrup over a pan of clean snow to make maple sugar wax.

Following 54 years of educational work, his last 24 as the superintendent of the Second Supervisory District of Herkimer County, Silas retired in 1936. During retirement, he spent a great deal of time writing. Regional history of the early Herkimer County settlers and his youthful days were favorite topics.

The following excerpt is taken from the second of a three-part series he wrote that was published in the Spring 1954 issue of *North Country Life* magazine.

"The sweetest and most popular of all of Gram's get-togethers were her jack wax parties. In April the young people would begin to tease Gram not to forget her annual jack wax party. When the most convenient date for all concerned was set, the hired boy would fill two or three milk cans with clean snow which he dug out of the interior of the big snow bank over in the hollow. No invitations were sent. All the young people of the immediate neighborhood were welcome to come. A large part of them were hired boys and hired girls on the nearby farms.

Lt. to Rt. Lyman and Milo Conklin. Boiling maple sap into syrup in the central Adirondacks about 1890. *Courtesy Edward Blankman (The Lloyd Blankman Collection)*

Sherriff Lake hunting camp. Many Adirondack woodsmen made a living as hunting and fishing guides, among other things. Sportspeople not only benefited from the service of their guide but appreciated hearty meals that often included recipes using locally-produced maple sugar. *Courtesy Piseco Historical Society*

"Each girl who came was expected to come with her 'feller' and bring a milk pan and two table forks. When the young people arrived, they would find Gram hovering over a couple of kettles of Gramp's maple syrup bubbling on the kitchen stove. At the cry of 'Snow, snow,' each couple would hasten to the hired boy's cans of snow. Each 'feller' would fill his girl's pan with snow and when Gram shouted 'Jack wax, jack wax,' each couple presented their pan of snow on which Gram spooned a covering of boiling

syrup which immediately cooled into the stickiest and sweetest substance ever conceived by nature.

"The couples would seat themselves about the room, facing one another with their pan on their laps, and begin to roll up forkfuls of that sticky nectar.

"When the guests could hold no more, each one was given a saucer and spoon and at the cry of 'Sugar, sugar,' they marched in single file past the kitchen stove while Gram filled each saucer with the hot syrup. The procession passed on out of doors, where each stirred and cooled his syrup till it became maple sugar. Each guest was expected to wrap it up in a piece of paper and take it home.

"The last act of the evening was to hug Gram for her goodness and labor—the boys wanted to but 'dassn't'-and the girls made Gramp blush by showering him with kisses to pay for his contribution of maple syrup."

Recipe | **Maple Drop Cookies**

Cream ½ cup butter and add 1 beaten egg, ¾ cup maple syrup and 2 tablespoons milk. Sift together 2 cups flour, 2 teaspoons baking powder, and ½ teaspoon salt. Add to these ingredients 1 cup chopped nuts and ½ cup raisins. Combine the two mixtures and drop by small spoonfuls on a greased pan. Bake in a moderate oven for 10 minutes.

Opposite: "Sugaring." Before modern methods eliminated some of the labor intensive work, sap was gathered in buckets hung on metal taps. Metal hoods kept out rain and debris. Sap was then gathered by hand, emptied into larger containers, and transported to a sugar shanty by horses pulling bob-sleighs. At shantys, the sap was transferred into a long vat where it was brought to a boil using wood heat under the flat pan to evaporate the sap. The resulting syrup was then cooled and stored in bottles or canned.
Author's photo taken at Norton's Family Farm

CHAPTER 10

Anna Brown's Adirondack Camp Cleaning Solutions

BETWEEN THE PAGES of these old North Country recipes was a clipping Anna must have found useful for help with cleaning. While these are old-fashioned cleaning methods using items commonly found around most homes, these money-saving ideas are staging a comeback in today's homes among those concerned with less exposure to strong chemicals. Anna might say, "What goes around comes around!"

ALL-PURPOSE CLEANERS
Vinegar and Salt. Mix together for a good surface cleaner.
Baking Soda. Dissolve 4 tablespoons baking soda in 1 quart warm water, or use baking soda on a damp sponge. Baking soda will clean and deodorize all kitchen and bathroom surfaces.
Vinegar. Dilute with water for general cleaning; use undiluted for tougher stains.
Lemon Juice. Dilute with water for general cleaning; use undiluted for tougher stains.
Washing Soda. Dilute 3 tablespoons per quart of warm water.

SCOURING POWDERS
Borax, Baking Soda or Table Salt. Sprinkle onto a damp sponge, scour and rinse. A paste of baking soda, salt and water also works as an oven cleaner.

Unidentified woman in kitchen. When house-cleaning time commenced, menfolk knew that they might just as well resign themselves to their wives' short tempers and to taking sketchy meals where and when they could. *Courtesy Special Collections, Feinberg Library, SUNY College of Plattsburgh*

DISINFECTANTS

Soap. Regular cleaning with plain soap and hot water will kill some bacteria.

Keep Surfaces Dry. Mold, mildew and bacteria cannot live without dampness.

Borax. Mix ½ cup Borax into 1 gallon of hot water. Borax long has been recognized for its disinfectant and deodorizing properties. However, borax, while a safer alternative than many products, is still toxic and should be kept out of the reach of children and pets.

City folks found Adirondack boarding houses offered the changes they needed from their hectic urban life. Old registers tell of their popularity. *Courtesy Piseco Historical Society*

DRAIN CLEANERS

Prevention. To avoid clogging drains, use a drain strainer to trap food particles and hair; collect grease in cans rather than pouring it down the drain; pour a kettle of boiling water down the drain weekly to melt fat that may be building up.

Baking Soda and Vinegar. Put ½ cup baking soda and ½ cup vinegar down the drain and cover the drain. Let sit for a few minutes, then pour a kettle of boiling water down the drain to flush it.

FURNITURE POLISHES

Olive Oil and Vinegar. Mix 3 parts oil to 1 part vinegar. Apply and polish with a clean, soft cloth.

Olive Oil and Lemon Juice. Mix 2 parts oil and 1 part lemon juice. Apply and polish with a soft cloth.

Water Spots. To remove water marks on furniture, rub gently with a cloth dipped in mayonnaise or vegetable oil. Allow it to sit overnight to penetrate the wood. Remove residue the next day. If mark is still visible, repeat.

BAKING SODA AND VINEGAR can be used to clean cooktops, which can seem totally resistant to everything else designed to clean them. Try vinegar and water (1:1) to wash pesticides off produce. Fill a fabric softener spray dispenser with straight vinegar to soften clothes and keep the washer free of odors. To cut hard water stains on glass shower doors, use a half lemon and baking soda. Use the lemon half as a "scrubber" and keep adding baking soda to the lemon half. Let stand for a few hours, then rinse. ❦

CHAPTER 11

The Brown's Camp and Garden Produce Meals

CHARLEY BROWN used to say, "I guess I was cut out to be a one-man hound dog, 'cause the only thing I really care 'bout is hunting." Then he would go on about how the Lord shorted him. "If I had four of them legs like old Redbone, instead of two, I could get 'round like the dickens."

Maybe he would have been able to. Rev. Byron-Curtiss never doubted Charley's sincerity. The fact is, though, that he couldn't have been a more disinterested spectator when civilization surrounded him. His longest employment was as North Lake's gatekeeper. This was one job that agreed with his slant on life, for it lacked set working hours and there wasn't actually much work to perform. There was no one around to tell him what to do and when to do the little work that the job did require. He rarely saw a supervisor. Housing was one of the perks of the job, and from Charley's point of view, what was even better was that a game-filled forest surrounded the headwaters of the Black River. And on top of all the peace and free time, Charley got a regular paycheck.

Charley always gave the impression he had no better place to go even on what someone else would consider a dull day. Rev. Byron-Curtiss once saw a few of the old boys around the lake plan a fishing trip with him. They showed up raring to head off, but Charley randomly "sailed around" — the preacher's term for wasting time doing absolutely nothing— so much so that by the time they got him started it was just about time to come home! His heart wasn't in fishing or working. In fact, it didn't seem as though it was in much of anything.

However easygoing Charley was, he and his wife, Anna, were committed vegetable gardeners. In fact, their garden plot was one of the largest open sunny spaces to be had at North Lake. Like other people of their generation, the Browns' collective garden experience was handed down from generation to generation and shared with neighbors and friends.

At the very heart of this story is an abiding reverence for Charley. That admiration is expressed in Rev. Byron-Curtiss' many tales that built up Charley's reputation. This is not a story of basic gardening at the Browns' camp or the couple's emphasis on building up the mountains' thin soil, feeding the earthworms, co-operating with nature, and concentrating on the fundamentals, although they did all that. This is a story about Charley,

The State House at North Lake, Atwell, N.Y. about 1890s. *Author's Collection*

because Charley was a character. It's followed by a few recipes Anna created from the bounty of their vegetable garden.

Charley was an inventor and professional procrastinator, and he was a genius at both. Those career fields require plenty of thinking time. The world will never know the hours and brain waves he invested in a device for removing old stumps from the shallow bottom of the reservoir at the State House landing where he docked boats. After thinking through all

Gardening provided an important supply of food for North Country people who relied on being as self-sufficient as possible. *Courtesy Town of Webb Historical Association*

Robert Knobel's North Lake camp, formerly owned by Charley and Anna Brown, located on the north side of the lake near the state line. 1939. Charley Brown was a long-time gate keeper of North Lake's reservoir. The left side is the original log cabin built by Owen "Kettle" Jones in the early 1890s. *Courtesy Thomas and Doris Kilbourn*

the angles of the stump-removal problem, he came up with a remarkably simple solution. At low water, Charley securely tied several air-tight oil drums to a stump, then waited for the water level to rise. Over time, nature completed the work. He had all sorts of what I thought were ingenious inventions. Rev. Byron-Curtiss' friend and author Thomas C. O'Donnell retells many of the local Charley Brown tales he learned from B-C in "Never a Dull Moment," found in *Birth of a River*.

O'Donnell tells a story about the day Charley asked Bob Bellinger to come over to Atwell to paint some boats. Bob needed to get his hay in, but he figured it could wait a day while he made a little extra money. What happened was that Charley kept getting sidetracked, and for two entire days Bob hung around waiting for instructions on painting the boats.

When hunting season opened, though, Charley was an entirely different person. Like an Olympic runner, he was at the starting line, on his toes and waiting for the starting gun.

Lib Bronson had Charley figured out pretty well. B-C said he would "never forget how she put it. I had bought a half-pound pouch of Warnick and Brown smoking tobacco for her. I always brought her a package of the tobacco when I stopped by to gossip, as I often did. Lib liked to smoke a pipe, but the home-cured black cordage she put in hers was so pungent that it left lurid memories in my head. Her tobacco smelled something like the burn of a slow fuse on a stick of dynamite. I know of a lumberjack who dropped in to see her husband, Wash. During their confab, Wash offered him a bowl of tobacco from Lib's tobacco box. Wash told me when that lumberjack left to return to camp he could hear him up over the hill, half a mile away, hollering 'Timber! Timber! Timber!'"

Lib and B-C would sit, rock and gossip for hours. Invariably the conversation would swing around to Charley Brown. Lib would always start by saying, "Charley's all right. He's the kind of man that just didn't ripen up and get meller 'til late in his fall."

Unidentified men in Anna Brown's kitchen. If there was anything that irritated Anna, it was to have Charley brag about his mother's cooking when he compared hers to his wife's culinary skills. In truth, a big slice from a well-browned and crusted loaf of Anna's homemade bread, or biscuits fresh from the oven, spread thick with homemade butter, jelly, or maybe sprinkled with brown sugar or touched lightly with maple syrup or molasses would garner the compliment, "Anna, I never tasted better. It'll stick to your ribs, boy! It'll stick to your ribs." *Author's Collection*

There are many legends about Charley's hunting ability, and most of them are true, including those about his marksmanship. Rev. Byron-Curtiss knew him for over twenty years and can attest to most of the tales. One summer when The Reverend had a touch of rheumatism, he recounted, "I was taking a 'sun treatment,' meaning I wasn't doing much in particular. At that time Charley managed a hotel in Morehouseville. Mind you, a hotel in Morehouseville had about as much business as an ice factory in Alaska. Nevertheless, I had got to thinking about Charley since he left the lake and had it in my mind to go see him. When I arrived, Charley, the main host and barkeep, seemed to be behind in his duties, as was always the case. I based my observation on the pile of glasses that were in need of washing at the bar."

"I caught an early dinner that afternoon and then came out to visit with him on the hotel porch. Charley's chair was tipped up on its two back legs, holding up one of the porch posts. He was staring off into the blue of the late afternoon sky; a faraway look was in his eyes. He made no amiable remark, but that did not surprise me. That pattern of non-acknowledgment was characteristic of the old woodsman. I noticed a crow perched on a dead pine stub, so I concentrated on the crow and soaked in the warm sunshine. Then, I heard the shrill scream of a hawk. Immediately I knew what Charley was watching so intently. The hawk was circling around high in the air. I followed it a while, then asked Charley, 'Know what he's after?'

"Charley waited about five minutes before answering. Pointing slowly to a cedar thicket on the side hill, he said softly, 'A young rabbit is playing 'round in them cedars.'

We sat for another spell in silence, watching the graceful soaring of the hawk far up in the sky. Only after a long lapse did I continue our limited conversation. 'Do you think he'll catch the rabbit?' It took Charley a while to figure that out. He shook his head and said, 'Not a chance. There's a crow's nest in that old spruce and them crows won't let him down.' "I always put stock in Charley's opinion in such matters."

Rev. Byron-Curtiss was about to change the conversation around a little by asking a question about the crows, but just then a man drove up with a dog in the back seat. The preacher continued, "He called to Charley by name—asked what kind of beer he had. Charley rattled off the brands he had in stock, but never once did he take his eyes off the hawk. Following his response the hawk let out a scream. The driver looked up in the sky and joined our stare as all three of us watched the large bird. After a spell the man turned to Charley and said, 'Do you think you could hit him, Charley?'

"Charley took quite a while to reply. But when he did he spoke with authority: 'Ain't got the right kind of ammunition.'

"The man looked at Charley, turned back toward the hawk, then returned his attention to Charley. 'How about a bottle of Budweiser?' he asked.

"Charley never batted so much as an eyelid. The man eyed him rather impatiently for many long silent minutes. The hawk screamed again. 'Look, Charley,' he said in a mildly exasperated tone. 'I'm a human being and I want a bottle of beer. I got me an errand down the line; set that beer out for me when you get time. I'll stop in and drink it on my way back.'"

O'Donnell explained that Charley and Rev. Byron-Curtiss watched the hawk and the crow for on to an hour or so. The man who had ordered the beer came back. "Charley eased himself away from the post and went into the bar room. The man and I followed. Charley went behind the bar, picked up a glass and began polishing it without a word. Then he noticed that someone had put the mail on the bar. He picked up each letter, examining the envelopes carefully on both sides.

"Just as he began to draw a jackknife from his pocket to open the letters, the now less-than-patient man's dog jumped out of the car and began approaching the open door." The man's dog was met by Charley's hound. "The two started a little argument on the front porch. All three of us exited the bar to see how the ruckus would come out. All along Charley kept polishing the beer mug. Following that excitement, we moved back into the bar room. During the interruption Charley discovered he had mislaid his jackknife. Not finding it right off, he had begun opening the letters with an ice pick when an obviously regular customer came through the side door, which Charley had left wide open. The regular's pickup was parked on the side street with a load of shoats in the back.

"Charley automatically put a bottle of what I assume was the man's 'usual' on the bar. The pair began to discuss pork while all along Charley continued polishing the same glass. When the pork problem was solved and the ice pick was discovered sticking in the doorjamb, Charley concentrated his full attention on opening his mail.

"The fellow who had been waiting for his beer finally became disgusted. He announced gruffly that if he couldn't get his beer, he might as well go to Salisbury for one. With that he turned, left the room and drove off. As his car sped down the road I glanced back at Charley. All he did was shrug, swipe the glass once or twice more, place it upside down on a pyramid of other turned-over glasses, rinse out another in the little sink and begin polishing that one. I was both amused and happy to see that Charley had not changed a bit since moving from North Lake."

The owner of Nat Foster Lodge was happy too that he had the opportunity to again sit at Mrs. Brown's table and be served a batch of her biscuits with wild honey and enjoy the kind of home-cooked food she had once served in the State House dining room. A few of Anna Brown's recipes follow.

Recipe   SEVEN LAYER MEAT & VEGETABLE DISH

Ingredients:
3 cups potatoes (cubed)
1 cup carrots (sliced?)
2 to 3 medium onions
1 can whole kernel corn, drained
1 cup rice
1 (16 ounces) can tomatoes
2 lbs. sausage or hamburger
Salt and pepper
Directions: In 3-quart casserole, layer potatoes, carrots, corn, onions, rice, salt and pepper to taste between layers. Arrange sausage or hamburger patties on top. [Anna mashed the tomatoes with a potato masher and poured it over the top.] Bake in oven at 375°F. for 1½ hours or until vegetables are tender.

Recipe   BAKED CUCUMBERS

Ingredients:
3 good-sized cucumbers
¾ cup fine dry bread crumbs
3 tablespoons butter
½ teaspoon salt

1½ tablespoons chopped onion

1½ teaspoons finely chopped parsley

1 tablespoon chopped celery

1 cup tomatoes cut in pieces

Directions: Wash cucumbers and cut in half lengthwise. Scoop out as much as possible of the pulp without breaking the skin. Brown the onion in the fat; add other ingredients mixed with the cucumber pulp. Stir constantly and cook 5 minutes, or until dry. Place the filling in the cucumber shells and bake until shells are soft and the mixture is brown on top.

The author's wife's prescription after working in the garden is take a lakeside hammock break with a good book. *Photograph by author*

CHAPTER 12

Old Fashioned Recipes & Cures

ONE WEEKEND, as I was welding a go-devil, a wood splitting axe, at my Adirondack facsimile lean-to, I thought about all the labor it took to cut, split, stack, and dry wood for heating and cooking back in the day. I had thoughts too of the unusual-sounding old recipes I'd read in camp cookbooks or heard mentioned. Certainly most dishes had been cooked on a wood-fired kitchen cookstove, although I know for a fact that Doc Latimer, Camp Seward's renowned chef-owner, relied on a reflector oven, sometimes known as a portable stove-top oven, to bake pies and cakes. He'd set it on top of the cast iron lids on Camp Seward's boxstove, where it would reflect heat. Doc didn't have a formal camp book of recipes. I learned about his cooking talents from his son, who was also a family physician. Probably because they were doctors, the men were also interested in cures that sound startling today. Who today would even think of putting a mixture of moss scraped from stones and simmered in cream in their mouth for a cold sore?

I would have had no idea what an attack of the ague was, or that wearing a piece of frankincense around one's neck was the standard cure, except that a friend's grandfather, Tom O'Donnell, mentioned it in his diary. He wrote about one incident when his friends had arrived to see him. "…I was in the midst of all this when relief came: my regular visitation of shaking ague. Old Pat took over the job of discouraging potato bugs. John Wilsey, who had never believed in so much as the existence of the disease, came

The author working up firewood. *Author's Collection*

in to see me in the grip of the ague, and by good chance at a time when I was putting on one of my more brilliant exhibitions. He looked on in silence at my performance. When the attack was over and the bed had ceased rattling, he said, 'Gee but that was fun. Do it again, Tom!'"

"…John was asking what started the ague anyhow, and I told him potato bugs. Just one of my casual observations…"

Of course Tom was joking. The violent shakes were brought on by a fever. The cure? Mix one pound of blue vervain stalks and 4 ounces of boneset in with a gallon of good Irish whiskey. One teaspoon three times a day should bring the fever or ague under control.

Another cure out of the past was to wear finely pulverized rock salt between the feet and the stockings for athlete's foot. The remedy for worms was a teaspoon to a tablespoon of garlic dissolved in Irish whiskey and taken every morning.

Wormwood tea or taking a bath in beef's brine was recommended for rheumatism. A standard cure for the croup was equal quantities of mustard and salt mixed in a half glass of water, or even better, lard and molasses, skunk's oil and alum in water!

One-half pound of lean beef chopped fine added to one-half pint of rain water, a half teaspoon of salt and four drops of muriatic acid was supposed to be good for indigestion and diarrhea, but only after it stood for three hours. Then the clear liquid was taken after it was strained through a cloth.

Here is an odd "Corrective for the Stomach:" a small piece of lime soaked in a quart of boiling water with a handful of raisins, with the dish kept covered while decomposition was taking place.

A remedy for burns was a poultice made from soot taken from the inside of a stove pipe or chimney and one to three parts lard or fresh butter. This mixture was then spread on linen or muslin and applied to the burn.

The following is taken from an old *Malone Cookbook* loaned to Genevieve L. Wood by Mrs. Charles Anderson of Gouverneur. The date of publication is not known.

"Cure for Felon:[5] Take equal parts of soft soap and best plug tobacco and simmer together. While hot bind on finger. It is frequently necessary for the patient to take a stimulant when this is applied."

Our ancestors were hardy folk.
They lived no life of ease,
But the cures they used for the ills they had
Were worse than the disease.

—From an unknown poet

Maybe there was some value to these cures in the past, but I wouldn't trust them. And, no one reading them should. There are far safer corrective measures today. I would far rather sample some of the old recipes that have equally strange names, such as Glazed Currants and Graham Pudding.

The pudding was easy to make in camp: 1 cup of molasses, 1 cup of milk, 2 cups of graham [whole wheat] flour, 1 cup of raisins, 1 saltspoon[6] of salt, 2 teaspoons of soda. Mix these ingredients and steam two hours.

Who today would look forward to a meal of fried cabbage? Its directions: "Chop fine a small cabbage. Put it in a frying skillet with water enough to cover and cook until tender. Then add 1 teaspoon of sweet cream, a piece of butter the size of an egg, pepper and salt. Fry till nearly dry. Serve hot." I'd far rather look forward to some pickled cabbage, or better yet, pickled fish.

Recipe   **PICKLED FISH**

Put the fish in vinegar that is spiced as for pickles. Boil slowly until tender but not broken. Set away closely covered, and in a few weeks the bones will be destroyed.

Recipe   **PIONEER BREAD MADE OF WOOD**

As unconventional as these dishes seem today, they pale in comparison to Bread Made of Wood. This recipe was discovered in the *Farmers' and Emigrants' Handbook*, 1845. The tome was "dedicated to John Jacob Astor of New York, an Emigrant from the Rhine."

In times of great scarcity, and where famine threatens, it is well to know how to prepare a nutritious substance, which may go under the name of bread, from the beech and other woods destitute of turpentine.

    Take green wood, chop it into very small chips, or make it into shavings, which is better. Boil these three or four times, stirring them very hard during boiling. Dry them, and reduce them to powder if possible; if not, as fine as you can. Bake this powder in the oven 3 or 4 times and then grind it as you would corn. Wood thus prepared acquires the smell and taste of corn flour. It will not ferment without the addition of leaven. The leaven prepared for corn flour is the best to use with it.

It will form a spongy bread, and when much baked with a hard crust is by no means unpalatable.

This kind of flour boiled in water and left to stand, forms a thick, tough trembling jelly, which is very nutritious, and in times of scarcity may be used to restore life, with perfect confidence.

I've thought as I have worked at my woodpile that it's quite possible many Americans today have never chopped wood. Likewise, a good majority of

1946. Frank Skillman at Camp Seward. Doc Latimer's Cold River camp was the site for many wilderness gourmet-style meals. *Photographer C.V. Latimer, Sr., M.D. Courtesy C.V. Latimer Jr., M.D.*

folks might not be able to identify varieties of wood: beech, soft and hard maple, white and red oak, basswood, cherry, and locust, for instance. It all has to do with the needs and exposures of one's life. I enjoy working up stacks of firewood. The very progress cheers me on. However, I'm glad I have never had to make bread from wood!

When I stayed at Camp Oasis, I learned from my grandparents how to split stove wood with a hatchet without cutting my fingers off. I must have been only six or seven years old. Later I learned the rudiments of how to maintain a wood-burning range. Watching Grandma cook on the cast iron stove-top range was a big thing. It took experience, skill and a bit of knack to boil something over one stove lid, simmer something over another, and keep something warm over still another, all at the same time and with the same fire.

Those cooking techniques have gone by the wayside for the most part.

There are those little Everhot ovens that will bake a cake over a campfire. An outdoor grill would work too, but why bother when the modern kitchen electric or gas oven is so much easier?

My wife and I still bake up some of our grandmothers' tasty breads in our kitchen today. I'm always amazed by how fast a loaf of wholesome bread disappears. Bread-on-a-stick is about all I'll bother cooking over an outdoor fire when camping. While the old cookbooks I've collected contain oodles of period recipes—Confederate Army Soup, Hickory Nut Pie, Green Corn Patties, Tomato Jam, Spruce Beer, and Parsnip Fritters—one of my favorites—it's not the cooking lore that pulls my mind back to camp days gone by. It's the tales that *don't stretch the blanket too far.* 🐟

© Natika / Dollar Photo Club

CHAPTER 13

Adirondack Spring Trout and Strawberry Pancakes

"GOOD HEAVENS, your Troutship," exclaimed a blinking Earl Fuller, a medical doctor from Utica, as the Rev. Byron-Curtiss drew in on the cotton line and netted a beautiful two-pound brook trout wagging a well-crisped fin. "You caught a beauty on that old peeled alder sapling pole this time."

Earl managed to get up to Nat Foster Lodge at least once every fly-fishing season. He considered fly-fishing for brook trout to be "first-rate sport." He was thankful there were so many good trout streams between the southwestern Adirondacks and the Mohawk Valley.

The Reverend and Earl shared a love for warm sun and tiny wild strawberries added to their pancakes, and a tolerance for the ferocious little black flies that caused them to swat and scratch their itching skin, bitten right through their shirts. Fishing near Nat Foster Lodge, the duo used to cut over the hill and take an old woods road up over the mountain, striking Grindstone Creek where it began coursing down a long wooded, rocky slope—all rips, falls, and deep pools, one after the other. The water was so turbulent that you could just as well fish downstream as up, as far as the trout were concerned, and it was a heap easier. Besides, when they quit fishing they had only a short walk to a trail that led back to the camp.

One day, as the men were going down the trail from the brook, after several hours of fishing, they met Raymond F. Dunham and Harvey ("Rascal"), his brother, both of Utica, who had also been fishing up in North

April 1, 1959. First day of trout fishing for two unidentified Old Forge gals who could not wait for the snow to melt before dipping their lines into an Adirondack lake. *Courtesy Town of Webb Historical Association*

Lake country. As they walked downhill toward the Bob Jones trail they showed each other their creels.

"Don't run as large as they once did," B-C said to Raymond.

"Maybe not," he replied, "but sometimes the big ones will take a fly when they won't look at a red wiggler."

"Maybe the big ones just got away from you, Raymond. Seems as though there ought to be big trout in the pools along the headwaters streams."

Raymond was used to Rev. Byron-Curtiss's good-natured ribbing. It mattered little that he was in the company of the clergy; he always gave Byron an unvarnished image (and more) of his outdoor adventures with the Dominie.

"'Spose I watch you try a couple of casts again, Your Eminence—long as you don't make for an old stump like the last time," referring to a fishing trip the crew had taken at Mud Pond.

"That's just not fair! It was a long cast, and before I could take in the slack, the line snagged over a root."

"Well, sir, I was just plum disgusted at such a poor showing of fishing, Byron. It was a good thing youthful Rascal was along so's he could wade right out and free your snagged line! There might have been a fairly large trout on the hook, but if'n you don't land 'em, the ones that get away don't count."

"Let me tell you a story," the preacher said as he turned to Rascal. "Besides being a minister, I have many other callings up north. Some of them have brought me quite a lot of attention and perhaps a good reputation. Still, now and then I do have a certain number of unprofitable fishing days. But the day I was out with the Franklin people wasn't one of those times. I'm going to get up and tell you a regular fishing story."

At that, Raymond's pal broke into a tale that "Rascal" still recalled decades later when outstretched before a crackling fire of pine knots, breathing the invigorating mountain air, listening to the soft murmur among the pines high overhead, as he and The Reverend shared some of the memories and the joy of living in the Adirondacks. This retelling is The Reverend's account of an interesting night-time fishing experience.

This particular night I'm telling you about, the bullheads were jumping pretty unconstrainedly. Free as the breeze, you might say, when they seen the light of our campfire blaze and the yellow glow of kerosene lanterns hooked on poles near the bank. Seems they fell all over themselves leaping for the bait. We had a fair-sized pile by the time six o'clock in the morning came around. Some folks fish in the evening and night. I think between four and seven a.m. is the best period. In the early morning hours they feed in the riffles and just below fast-water stretches—under large rocks, submerged logs and roots.

We pushed out the old Yankee pine-plank boat and drifted to the best spot for a final go at them near the inlet of Lily Lake. If we'd been wise we would have snuffed out our light. But we weren't smart.

Well, when we came into the cold fast-water stretch of that feeder creek, the rain of bullheads into the boat was something awful. There were fish everywhere feeding like pigs in a trough. We used a fairly short bait-casting rig with a linen line of 14- to 18-pound test. Many fishermen know the fun of bullhead fishing, but that morning will rank with the best. You should have seen those large-headed fishes as they began to jump for the size 1/0 to 4/0 hooks. One fish that weighed 10 pounds after we dressed him made a spring and struck his big head directly into my kneecap. He was so infernally incensed at having his merriment fumbled that he opened his jaws and took a bite of my leg. That mischief made me limp for two weeks. He was nasty.

Within minutes the fish began to come in so fast that the boat began to sink. I yelled to Joseph, "Bail out! We're going to draw this boat ashore before we lose the fish." By this time the boat had settled to the spreader. We jumped ship just in time to save her from sinking. Luckily the water wasn't very deep, making it easy for us to beach the craft, but by the time we got her there the boat was so full that the pile of fish was sliding over the gunwales.

We sat up on the shore for a couple of hours and cleaned that prize catch of fish. Then we pitched the prize lot of them back into the boat.

As none of them had any innards, they didn't weigh as much as before. But we blew out the light so none of the bullheads left in the water would bother us on our way to the landing.

Once we arrived home we weighed those fish on the State House scales and found those bullheads weighed an even five hundred pounds, dressed!

Some folks see a sight of difference between fishing and angling. They'll tell you that a true angler never uses bait—nothing but flies and other artificial lures. That's right fine sentiment. But somehow, it seems as though we'd be missing a heap of sport if we couldn't worm it once in a while. No sir, I'm not a mite ashamed to use the good old worm.

This is but one of the countless fishing tales told around campfires and cook stoves—tales that were almost as much fun as the fishing trips themselves, and especially enjoyable because they could be told again and again, and with endless variations.

Fishing Adirondack waters has been a favorite pastime for men and women Adirondackers and the throngs of visitors who frequent the mountains. Rev. Byron-Curtiss stands by his party's one day legal-sized catch. Circa 1930s. *Courtesy Thomas and Doris Kilbourn (The A. L. Byron-Curtiss Collection)*

The plump bullhead, the woven pack basket, and talk of late spring night fishing belong to the years passing in review. "Rascal" Dunham sighed not for the fishing, but for the flavor of the years past and for other sweet echoes of camping in the Adirondacks.

In the years to come, Rascal would return often to reminisce with the Bishop of North Lake. With his thirty years of collecting first-hand information, Harvey L. Dunham would go on to write *Adirondack French Louie,* a classic example of Adirondack literature.

Surely during his visits with Rev. Byron-Curtiss, he enjoyed the preacher's fruit pies. Regardless of which fruit was available—just-picked wild blueberries or the first apples of an upstate autumn, perhaps—everything tasted good in this unusual crust. And that is no stretch of the truth!

Recipe ## NAT FOSTER LODGE GALETTE PASTRY

The baker notes this pastry is used for open fruit pies, cooked, canned or fresh, such as plum, peach, apple, blueberry, cherry, and strawberry. Sprinkle fruit with sugar if needed. Line pan with ¼ in. thick pastry. Fill with fruit. Bake 25 minutes at 425°F. An alternative is to make individual tarts.

The pastry: Sift 1 cup flour with ½ teaspoon salt & 1 tablespoon sugar. Cut in 6 tablespoons butter. Beat 1 egg yolk with 1 tablespoon water & 1½ tablespoons lemon juice & stir it in. Pat together and chill. Roll ¼ inch thick and fit into tin. Makes enough to fill 3 pie tins.

Recipe ## TRADITIONAL PANCAKES

Kitchen-tested tip: Add wild strawberries or blueberries for a delicious variation to these light, tasty griddlecakes.

Ingredients:

1¼ cups flour.

3 teaspoons baking powder.

1 tablespoon sugar.

½ teaspoon salt (optional).

1 beaten egg.

1 cup milk.

2 tablespoons canola oil.

Directions: Blend together dry ingredients. Combine egg, milk, and oil; add to dry ingredients, stirring just until moistened. Bake on hot griddle. Make about eight 4-inch pancakes. 🍶

Hardscrabble (Engineer) Lake in the southwestern Adirondacks. The remote location was once a popular water that drew anglers who returned with overflowing fish baskets. Today it makes a challenging and rewarding bushwhack. *Photograph by author*

CHAPTER 14

Berry Picking

THE DAY Rev. Byron-Curtiss's niece, Fran Woerpel and I drove to North Lake, we noticed thick patches of red and black raspberries growing in sunny clearings. It brought on a rush of the joy she experienced when berry-picking at camp.

Some campers liked to lounge, others liked to fish or row on the lake, but the adventurous went berrying in the lumber slashing.

Wild berries are an important food item in woodland animals' diets. They are equally as important to a hungry camper willing to accept scratches and torn clothing when she tackles thickly intertwined thorny brambles to gather enough plump fruit to bake a big golden-crusted pie or make a luscious wild berry shortcake.

Fran was only a little girl, but the berry-patch adventures of youth had not faded. She recounted one bright summer day back in those carefree years when she, with her mother, several aunts, and Uncle William, along with other siblings, rode in Uncle Arthur Byron's big boat to the head of North Lake to pick berries.

Fran was too young to think the outing was going to be work. She recalled, "I enjoyed the *rurring* sound of the outboard motor as it skimmed the boat over the surface of the water, and the short walk to a favored lumber slashing. The adults carried large milk and smaller lard pails. The children carried coffee tins. Two holes, punched opposite each other, had been fashioned into the cylinder's walls. A long string looped over our necks and knotted on the insides of the cans allowed us to carry the cans effortlessly. It also made it easier for small outstretched hands to pluck the fat brooches of black jewels.

"You have to have had some experience in camp living to know what I mean when I speak of the uttermost happiness, the glance of true contentment, that comes over a child who is among thick patches of wild strawberries, surrounded by bushes heavy with clumps of blueberries or picking raspberries in a slashing. Fresh air, bird songs, and the hum of the natural world surround them. Besides fishing, I don't think there is another place I've been where I can feel so much joy as in a fruit-filled field or berry patch.

"I can still recall hearing my grandmother telling me how to use my thumbnail to cull the green tops of strawberries as I picked to save preparation time once home. I can remember the immediate pain from the prick of tiny thorns that would pierce my skin as I reached underneath the berry leaves to gather clumps of fruit close to the canes that might have gone unnoticed by a less observant picker.

Fran and Robert Woerpel, Spring 2004. "The first time I believe I was at Nat Foster Lodge was in 1934. I was five years old. Rev. Byron-Curtiss baptized my cousin Allan at his outdoor chapel. "'Dear' was Rev. Byron-Curtiss' favorite way to address all of the children." *Author's Collection*

"Picking," said Fran, "was often a contest for me. I did not dawdle. 'I'll fill my basket before you,' I can hear myself say to my sister, who stood nearby resting and eating the majority of berries she had picked. Knowing that further treasure awaited me through the maze of brambles spurred me on. 'Go ahead. Get all scratched up,' she would reply with lips and teeth purple with juice.

"Even the annoying deer flies that buzzed around my head were a part of the picture. I also looked forward to a delicious shortcake topped with whipped cream, and jam to spread on toast. No taste of the treats that followed picking, however, could equal popping fresh berries into my mouth."

Fran, too, was thrilled when she happened onto a fine patch of blackberries, where in short order she could fill her pail, dump the contents into a larger water pail, and then fill her smaller pail again and again, hoping her sister Marcia and her cousins were not spotting quite so many clusters of berries as she was, so she could beat them.

Thanks to many hands, the picking party's pails filled quickly, and they left the clearing where once a forest had stood before the axe and crosscut saw of the lumbermen cleared it. Loaded into the boat, the full pails might have looked like a great achievement for youngsters.

Old Camp 5, Ice Cave Mountain. Circa 1910. Red and blackberry brambles grew up in former lumber camp clearings. *Courtesy Roy E. Wires (The Emily Mitchell Wires Collection)*

Spring Trout & Strawberry Pancakes: Borrowed Tales, Quirky Cures, Camp Recipes

Rev. Byron-Curtiss had a variety of boats he used to transport people over the water.
Courtesy Roy E. Wires (The Emily Mitchell Wires Collection)

Back at Nat Foster Lodge, the children grabbed a slice of buttered bread, then jumped endless times off the dock into the lake while their mothers prepared the evening meal and the anticipated dessert.

★ ★ ★

I HAVE FOUND many small patches of berries hemmed in by the encroaching forest, throughout the Adirondacks. Five years ago I discovered a few berry canes growing in a sunny clearing on the north shore of Mud Pond. Perhaps they germinated from seeds from a bird passing over—an unknowing "Johnny Appleseed bird." Some of the seeds sprouted into strong plants.

I've sat under the verandah at Byron-Curtiss's former camp, picturing him sitting there at an earlier time with his ever-present pipe in hand. I've thought of the snapshots shared with me that were taken at Nat Foster Lodge. I've imagined him saying to Fran, "You look as if you have had a happy afternoon berrying. Well, were you right? Did you pick the most berries?" According to Fran's memories, she must have proudly replied, "I did!"

Recipe   **FRAN'S STRAWBERRY SHORTCAKE**

What could be more delicious than delicate shortcake, fresh red ripe strawberries, and fluffy whipped cream?

2 cups flour.

2 tablespoons sugar (rounded).

3 teaspoons baking powder.

1 teaspoon salt (optional).

Blend in 6 tablespoons shortening.

(or substitute butter or margarine).

Mix in ⅔ cup milk (or substitute light cream).

1 beaten egg (optional).

Use a biscuit cutter or spoon into ungreased 9" x12" pan.

Makes about a dozen medium-sized shortcake biscuits.

Oven 450°F.

Time 10–12 minutes.

Recipe   **CAMP 7 STRAWBERRY SUNSHINE PRESERVES**

1 quart of stemmed strawberries.

4 cups of sugar.

Directions: Cook the fruit without sugar for 3 minutes. Add 2 cups of sugar and cook for 3 more minutes. Add 2 more cups of sugar and cook for 3 minutes longer. Pour into an earthen crock. Stir occasionally. In 3 days pack in jars and seal cold.

Recipe   **GRANDMA HELEN'S STRAWBERRY JELLO® CREAM PIE**

One 3 ounce package strawberry Jello®.

1¼ cups boiling water.

¼ cup sugar.

Dissolve Jello® and sugar in water then add 1 lb. frozen package of strawberries. Stir often at first, then occasionally. Cream ⅓ cup confectioner's sugar and 3 ounce package cream cheese. Fold in ½ pint whipped cream.

Directions: When strawberry mixture is thickened enough, layer with strawberry mixture first, then whipped cream cheese mixture in a baked nine-inch pie shell. Alternate layers, ending with strawberry mixture. Top with whipped cream. Chill until served. 🍸

Circa 1930s. A Linn tractor pulls into Camp VII, Ice Cave Mountain. Decades of logging in the southwestern Adirondacks has created pockets of open clearings perfect for today's pickers willing to do a bit of hiking to fill their pails with delicious wild berries. *Courtesy of Dorothy Payton*

SECTION THREE

Mountain Camp Kitchens, People and What They "Et"

THROUGH VISITS with older folks and campers, I changed a long-fixed view about food tastes. Grandma maintained all homemade butter was not always sweet and good, and visitors who drank Adirondack hermit Noah John Rondeau's coffee reported the brew was often boiled too long so that it was bitter and strong and could be drunk only after plenty of cream and sufficient sugar had been poured and stirred into the cup.

I still have a vivid picture of Mother's face, contorted from standing over a smoking campfire on a hot summer day, as she baked pancakes on a large cast iron griddle. Dad flipped the cakes into the air and onto my plate. I could hog down those griddle cakes faster than Mom and Dad could bake them.

The "vittles" that came out of early Adirondack cabin kitchens, such as the Twitchell camp, surely were not as well-balanced as the food prepared in the updated kitchens that would eventually come about as innovative improvements in cooking technology developed. Perhaps the food of our forefathers didn't taste as good, but the hard work it took to survive made for prodigious appetites.

Food preparation in the first cabin on Twitchell Lake involved rustic cooking equipment and utensils. *Courtesy Town of Webb Historical Society*

Later camp kitchens provided a host of improvements in equipment and tools of the trade that elevated working conditions for homemakers. *Karen Foley Photo/Dollar Photo Club*

CHAPTER 15

Twin Mountain Muffins and Lake Placid Blueberry Buckle

BETTE AND I ENJOY baked goods following our return from Sunday church service. The following recipes are family winners that we have accumulated from camp cookbooks. "Twin Mountain Muffins" was one of the first we tried from Nat Foster Lodge's book because it sounded woodsy. A notation next to the title indicates it came from "Miss Hurd" and emphasized "All level measurements."

Recipe **TWIN MOUNTAIN MUFFINS**

4 tablespoons butter.

½ cup sugar.

1 egg.

¾ cup milk.

2 cups pastry flour.

3 tablespoons baking powder.

Folded in quarters, clipped together with a rusty paper clip and stored in the bottom of a box of Rev. Byron-Curtiss' papers that included "Molasses Brownies," "Doughnuts—(Crisco can recipe)" and "Pork Cake," was a story of investigating the Adirondack Mountains in 1883.

Rev. Byron-Curtiss clipped a hand-written note to the typed story. It reads in part: "This is an account of Irving and Everett Johnson who made a trip on foot from North Creek to the top of Mount Marcy and from there to

Adirondack Lodge and through Indian Pass back to North Creek. It was the year that sixteen-year old Irving entered Union College and that twenty-six year old Everett was ordained a priest. They set out first by train from their mother's home in Schenectady, New York, heading for North Creek. Everett recalled, 'We had woven Adirondack pack baskets which we weighed with our loads and found each to weigh about fifty pounds. On this trip we carried no tent, very few cooking vessels, a light 32-caliber Remington rifle, a little fishing tackle, but no poles. Our chief load being made of provisions of the simplest kind —no canned stuff.'"

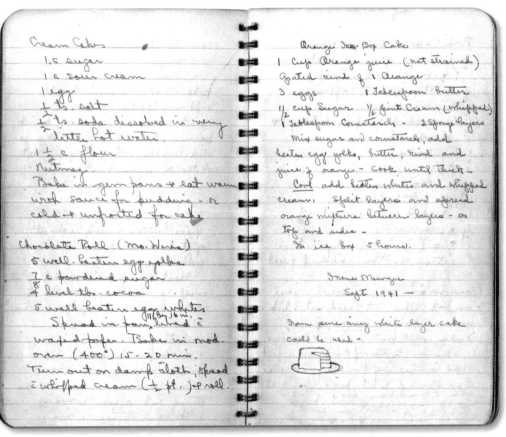

Handwritten recipe books, letters and post cards, oral storytelling, journals, diaries, photographs, and scrapbooks are excellent sources of primary information. Archived correctly, they retain history for future generations and provide an avenue to learn about the past. *Author's Collection. Courtesy of Roy E. Wires*

The blueberry buckle is a tried-and-true camp favorite.

Recipe   **LAKE PLACID BLUEBERRY BUCKLE**

½ cup of shortening.

¾ cup sugar.

1 egg.

2 cups sifted all-purpose flour.

2½ teaspoons baking powder.

¼ teaspoon salt.

½ cup milk.

2 cups fresh blueberries

Crumbly Topping

½ cup sugar.

½ cup sifted all-purpose flour.

½ teaspoon ground cinnamon.

¼ cup butter.

The beginning of the 20th century saw urban people buying land for cottages and establishing themselves as summer residents at any number of Adirondack lakes.
Courtesy Piseco Historical Society

A comfortable cottage interior. Old cookbooks found in long-standing camps offer a record of the recipes of the time period. *Courtesy Piseco Historical Society*

Directions: Thoroughly cream shortening and ¾ cup sugar; add egg and beat till light and fluffy. Sift together 2 cups flour, baking powder, and salt; add to creamed mixture alternately with milk. Spread in greased 11 x 7 x 1 ½-inch pan. Top with berries. Mix ½ cup sugar, ½ cup flour, and cinnamon; cut in butter till crumbly; sprinkle over berries. Bake at 350°F. for 45 minutes. Cut in squares. Serve warm. 🍶

CHAPTER 16

Frogging Grounds

TO REACH LILLY LAKE, Woodhull Lake, Twin Lakes, South Lake, or Little Salmon Lake and their most excellent frog bogs, one must follow old logging track roads, cross streams, climb over low mountains, and in some cases catch the infrequent once-blazed trails that have not been kept up to date.

These bodies of water are easy destinations I have enjoyed leading friends to. One needs to carry only a lightly-loaded pack basket, no camp baggage or other weighty accoutrements. They are day trips.

I don't think there is as much sport in frogging as there is in fishing or hunting, but frogs are well worth catching. As a youngster I was often guided to a favorite frogging ground by my grandfather. One old-timer used to extol the best things about frogging: "I don't imagine there's anything much better for a supper than fried frog legs, bacon, cornbread, and boiled coffee."

I never much cared for frog legs. My grandfather and father did. However, I did enjoy catching frogs.

Frogs are easy to catch. The only thing really needed is a boat or raft to pole among the lily pads. Frogs can be caught with cupped hands, in nets, or on small hooks baited with bits of red flannel. What little sport is derived from the hunt comes from dangling the red fabric bait in front of the smooth-skinned web-footed amphibians, or seeing them snatch at a red ibis artificial fly, which generally does the trick just as well. At night frogs are picked up with the aid of a light. "Just hold a light beam on their eyes, paddle alongside, and pick them up," were the first directions I remember hearing.

Reverend Byron-Curtiss was an avid sportsman, not a recreational hiker. His investigations usually focused on food-gathering, and he rowed boats rather than walking whenever possible.

South Lake and its surrounding wetland was my most routine destination when leaving Nat Foster Lodge. The approach to the lake unveils a quiet wilderness view of green woods, the odor of balsam and sweet-smelling cedar. A grand lily-padded shallow scene opens to the north at the end of the final downhill grade. To the south, a muddy tote road of sorts skirts the perimeter of the lake. It leads to an earthen dam. The old road forks beyond the dam. A sharp bushwhacker, by eyeing the faint evidence and employing good orienteering skills, can trace the old pathway paralleling Raymond Brook. (It leads to posted Adirondack League Club land.) The southbound fork is a New York State marked trail. It zigs across wet terrain, crosses Little Salmon Lake outlet and continues west, making a beeline toward West Canada Creek.

Rowing to the camp dock, the mates are smiling as they return with a full frogging basket. *Courtesy Thomas and Doris Kilbourn (The A. L. Byron-Curtiss Collection)*

Sometimes battered and fried, sometimes grilled, sometimes cooked on a spit over an open fire, frog legs are a delicacy eaten around the world, and a favorite of woodsmen in the Northeast United States. © *Monkey Business / Dollar Photo Club*

The wild east bay and the wetland along Raymond Brook were favorite frog-gathering spots. The Raymond Brook channel was once easier to travel than it is today. During B-C's heyday, the water route to Adirondack League Club property along Raymond Brook was not always restricted to nonmembers. The Reverend often secured and carried a pass in his pocket. The paper, provided by Utica friends who were ALC members, gave him permission to access their property.

The acreage around portions of South Lake is low and wet, still as picturesque as it was a century and more ago. High above the trees, mountain song birds pipe their notes. This was true frogging country in Rev. Byron-Curtiss's time. His log books are witness to the many parties that returned from it with a fine mess of bull frogs.

June 26, 1911
Charlie Raffany took a cold plunge and had to be thawed out for the next three hours. We took trip up the lake in the morning. In the afternoon we went to South Lake and secured a number of frogs which we had for supper. —A.L. B-C

Late autumn in the Adirondacks brings on a glorious calm. On those sunny days with a clear blue-sky atmosphere I try to head into the mountains. North Lake country is one of the closest destinations to drive to. I like the lake and forest backdrop. There is no clatter from the few cottages still occupied and generally no tents are pitched along the shoreline.

Anticipating the comfortable environs as I worked on this chapter's ending, I decided to stir up a batch of my favorite coffee cake for a snack and head to the woods around South Lake.

There are ruins of three sluice dams in the area. Two were from Gig Perry's days. The other was the Canahans' dam. That was located on the South Branch outlet about one mile from South Lake State Dam. All the lumbermen's dams have rotted away, but once I finished my thermos of coffee and ate the coffee cake I had packed, I decided I would make the site of Canahan's dam my destination for the day's hike. Since I have never called my grandmother's recipe anything but Favorite Coffee Cake, I decided to award it this title in honor of my day trip.

WOODLAND COFFEE CAKE

Ingredients:

¾ cup sugar.

¼ cup shortening.

1 egg.

½ cup milk.

1½ cups flour.

2 teaspoons baking powder.

½ teaspoon salt.

Directions: Mix sugar, short-ening, and egg thoroughly. Stir in milk. (More than what is called for might be needed.) Blend flour, baking powder, salt. Stir in mixture. Spread in a 9x9inch pan. Sprinkle on topping.

Topping: Blend ½ cup brown sugar with 1½ teaspoons cinnamon. (Optional: Add chopped walnuts). Bake at 375°F. for 25–35 minutes.

© *Brent Hofacker / Dollar Photo Club*

Opposite. Bill Pulling was 100% Adirondack. Born in Raquette Lake, Bill moved to Old Forge and ended up in Thendara. He began his career on the railroad, later moving on to become a carpenter. He loved to fish, go frogging, hunt, garden, and tell stories. Bill was never discouraged by the short, often forbidding growing season. He shared his enthusiasm for tending flowers and vegetables with his children, teaching them to fertilize the soil with all the little fish they caught so he didn't have to clean them. Bill would have loved to be a farmer, but in the Adirondacks it is hard to get much to grow. He maintained a vast rhubarb patch from which his wife Betty baked his favorite dessert—rhubarb crisp. Even if his garden wasn't successful, he'd spin a tale about his most victorious harvest—a nine-foot long zucchini. "Yes, it was quite a gauldang squash," would be about the way he'd bring up the preposterous vegetable. He considered hollowing it out and then fiberglassing the shell, thinking once he mounted a 10-horse outboard he'd be able to outrun any otter on the Moose River. *Courtesy Town of Webb Historical Association*

CHAPTER 17

The Sperrys' Yellow-Kid Camp and Taste-tested Breads

COOKBOOKS OFTEN ARE DIVIDED into sections that include appetizers, beverages, canning and preserving, pickle-making, meat, eggs, cheese dishes, salads, sandwiches, soups and vegetables, cookies, cakes, pies, breads, and desserts.

Recipes for bread, rolls, pies, and pastry reoccur in almost every Adirondack homemaker's cookbook, along with hand-written reminders such as: "Folding the top pie crust over the lower crust before crimping will keep the juices in the pie." "The cake is done when it shrinks slightly from the sides of the pan or if it springs back when touched lightly with the finger." And, what should be common sense, yet I've seen the reminder underlined: "Cakes should not be frosted until thoroughly cool."

In 1981 Charles and Claire Sperry self-published a fifty-four page book titled *North Lake: The Jewel of the Adirondacks.* They told me it was "a small history…written to try to preserve some of the names and experiences of earlier years."

Charles learned many names and local facts from his father and grandfather. He said their combined knowledge reached "back over one hundred years." Charles's personal experiences "started about 1910," he recalled.

During Charles and Claire Sperry's Adirondack camp life, they came to know all sorts of characters—crusty curmudgeons, freedom-loving trappers, an old-time silver miner, skillful guides, sporting folks, and loggers.

Spring Trout & Strawberry Pancakes: Borrowed Tales, Quirky Cures, Camp Recipes

In their youthful years they had traveled by horse and wagon over a tenuous dirt road to reach the Sperry camp. They had also traveled in the company of guides to outlying camps. The Sperrys took pride in their knowledge of woodcraft and their outdoor skills. One local family of guides they knew well were Dell, Arthur (who bore the nickname "Archie") and Fred Bellinger.

Charlie said one day while he was waiting on the Forestport railroad station platform, Archie Bellinger had come up to him and inquired about "going to The Reverend's camp at North Lake." Archie had known Rev. Byron-Curtiss for close to forty years. Rev. Byron-Curtiss later said he realized he was a marked man to Archie, for Archie had put forth the claim of knowing him before he was even born!

The Sperrys were camp neighbors. Charles and Claire maintained, "The Reverend had no enemies, not counting, of course, those deer and fish that were afraid of everybody, because they didn't want to end up in any human's fry pan."

Shortly after the event at the Forestport Station train depot, Byron-Curtiss was talking with the Sperrys. They were remembering Archie Bellinger. The Reverend had placed a cross by Archie's name in his camp journal to signify the guide's passing. He said of the guide, "Archie was blessed with a gift of gab that some said was even more impressive than Will Rogers."

Claire had brought The Reverend a loaf of homemade apple bread that day. She was using up the last of her stock of canned preserves. It wouldn't be long before a new apple harvest season began. And soon camp owners would set out for Sugar Loaf Mountain on the track of white-tail deer.

Rev. Byron-Curtiss noted the day reminded him of a similar day years earlier when a large flotilla of boats came toward the shore of Panther Bay. An assembly of people disembarked and made their way toward his camp. "They were stepping briskly with an earnest air as they shouted to me and waved their hands," he recalled. The Reverend was overjoyed. But, what did all these people want of him? His good company, a story—or coffee, fried cakes, bacon and trout?

He stood in calm dignity looking at them as they reached the top of the bank. Ben Beach, Jack Redmond, Archie Bellinger, and Ira Watkins's wife and child were the first to greet him.

"Can you preach fire and brimstone?" they asked almost in unison.

"Yes," he said, "you know I can, but not as well as the Vatican Pope," the preacher replied, surely wondering where this was heading.

"Yes, you can. We all know you can. And, because you can we have voted to give you the title of 'Bishop of North Lake.'"

The Reverend was tickled.

Archie offered, "We had talked about pinning the Pope of North Lake on you but decided you needed a more fitting title."

The label was indeed a prodigious honor. Rev. Byron-Curtiss told the gathering of neighbors they had made him feel very special but he didn't deserve it. He admitted, "I often exceed the daily limit of trout allowed by

Yellow-Kid Camp circa 1915. *Courtesy Bert Sperry*

law; the greater part of my fishing takes me onto posted land; and sometimes I indulge in over-consumption of 'wet goods.' So what would you say of all that?"

But they talked him beyond resistance, saying that nary a soul was more fair-minded, so he should accept this distinguished status. They would find no better man to bestow blessings on a fishing party, or for that matter, any kind of party, be it a picnic or food-gathering.

The story is just a neighborly account of the kind of reminiscing folks did at camp. Atwell was a small hamlet. Everyone knew each other. As each old-timer passed, his or her life seemed to be more embraced as they became part of the folklore of the Adirondack community.

I have included several favorite breads found in North Lake camp cookbooks. Claire's apple bread recipe is one of the best.

Recipe   **CLAIRE'S APPLE BREAD**

Ingredients:
½ cup sugar.
½ cup butter.
1 Tablespoon sour milk.
2 beaten eggs.
1 teaspoon vanilla extract.
2 cups flour.
1 teaspoon baking soda.
⅛ teaspoon salt.
1½ cups of chopped apples.

Directions: Cream sugar, butter, milk, eggs and vanilla. Add flour, soda, salt and apples. Grease baking loaf tin. Mix and spread topping consisting of 2 tablespoons sugar, 1 teaspoon cinnamon. Bake at 350°F. about 1 hour. Makes one large loaf or 2-3 mini-loaves.

The additional bread recipes that follow are attributed to Lib Brunson, Ma Getman, and Roselle Putney, all old-time Adirondack women who were residents of the Black River headwaters.

LIB BRUNSON'S PUMPKIN BREAD RECIPE

Ingredients:

4 eggs at room temperature.

3 cups sifted all-purpose flour.

2 teaspoons baking powder.

2 teaspoons baking soda.

1½ teaspoons cinnamon.

½ teaspoon ginger.

½ teaspoon nutmeg.

1 teaspoon salt.

2 cups sugar.

½ cup cooking oil.

One 14½ ounce can pureed pumpkin

(or same amount homemade).

1 cup raisins.

Directions: Sift together flour, baking powder, soda, spices and salt three times. Grease two loaf pans. Line the bottoms with buttered plain paper cut to fit. Preheat oven to 350°F. Mix oil and sugar thoroughly in large bowl. Add eggs one at a time, beating well after each addition. Begin and end with flour. Stir in raisins. Pour batter into pans. Bake for 1 hour, or until toothpick inserted in center comes out dry and clean. Cool on wire racks for 10 minutes. Remove from pans, peel off paper, and continue cooling.

Recipe **AUTUMN APPLE BREAD PIE!**

Ingredients:

½ cup flour

¾ cup sugar

2 large eggs

1 teaspoon baking powder

¼ teaspoon vanilla

1 cup diced apples

½ cup chopped nuts

Directions: Put flour, sugar, eggs in a bowl and mix. Add remaining ingredients. Pour into a 9-inch buttered pie plate. Bake 375°F. for 30 minutes. Serve with whipped cream.

Before arriving at camp Charles Sperry remembered his grandparents' first stop in Forestport would be, "the grocery store, where my grandfather would purchase the groceries that were necessary for our stay at camp." *Courtesy Thomas and Doris Kilbourn (The A. L. Byron-Curtiss Collection)*

CHAPTER 18

Atwell Martin's Chivalry

STORIES ABOUND throughout the greater Forestport community about Adirondack homesteaders Lib and Washington "Wash" Bronson. Lib and Wash operated a hostelry a couple of miles up from Farrtown, in the direction of Pony Bob's as one went out of the woods from Reed's Mill.

Lib and Wash were friends with Atwell Martin. Friendship set aside, Lib was surprised the day she and her sister invaded the privacy of Martin's hermitage when they had occasion to visit North Lake in the 1880s.

Lib wished to see her husband, who was working in Perry's lumber camp at the head of the lake. The women also purposed to pick some berries while in the area. Aware dark would overtake them, they stopped at Atwell's place, asking if they could spend the night in his woodshed.

Both women were familiar with the simplicities of woods etiquette, so since they planned to sleep in the woodshed, a bark affair in one corner of Atwell's clearing, they began to fix up a bunk with blankets they had carried. Atwell pitched in to help, gathering balsam boughs for their mattress, dry kindling for a fire and a fresh pail of water.

Lib reported Atwell's welcome "was restrained; though he consented that we prepare our supper on his stove." Although Atwell did commit to their sleeping in his woodshed "he did not enthuse over our plan." He consented to join them for supper, but "was silent and taciturn during the meal."

While the women washed the dishes, Atwell busied himself at three little tasks—Lib said, "forerunners of the strange course he was soon to follow."

When the women retired to the shed, Atwell was standing silently outside the door. As they entered the building, Atwell closed the door swiftly. They heard the rattle and snap of a padlock.

Naturally they were both astonished and startled; but before they had time to express it, Atwell said in his high-pitched voice, "Miss Brunson, be you all right?"

She spoke up and said, "Why, yes Atwell, we are all right, but what's got into you?"

His firm reply was, "Stop your yammerin' and let the other woman speak for herself, Miss." Whereat, Lib's sister answered, "Why, yes, Mr. Martin, we're all right." Then he proceeded to explain his strange action. "Folks about will talk," he said. "Now you wimmen, you've got wood and fresh water and the bed's made."

According to Rev. Byron-Curtiss, whenever she fished Lib Bronson was known to smoke a pipeful of her "pungent, home-cured black cordage" that was more powerful than a stick of dynamite. *Courtesy Thomas and Doris Kilbourn (The A. L. Byron-Curtiss Collection)*

Generations of campers were introduced to stories about Lib Bronson's experiences with Atwell. *Courtesy Thomas and Doris Kilbourn (The A. L. Byron-Curtiss Collection)*

Lib replied with outrage. "Nonsense, Atwell. The closest neighbors are the half dozen people in the reservoir tender's family nearly a half mile away through the forest, the men at a lumber camp a full two miles away or that old codger that lives three miles down the lake, and he's deafer than a hemlock stump."

Atwell turned quiet for a moment then replied, "Yes, Miss Brunson, but that old coot's got good eyes and he shore can talk, so you just keep still and everything will be all right."

"Unlock this door," Lib demanded. She was not at all happy with his decision to lock them in. "Where'd you get all them foolish notions, Atwell? You know me and my sister. We ain't got no designs on you."

Atwell wasn't about to concede. "Maybe you ain't up to no monkey business but you know how they like to put in the papers about them rendezvouses and clandestine assignations. I don't want no reputation like that."

The hermit was not about to take the chance of starting a local scandal, and Lib realized the conversation was getting too involved, so she switched over to the obvious question, "How be we going to get out of here?"

Atwell pondered, "I ain't come to that yet. You women just keep quiet until I get this thunk out."

"He puttered around," Lib told Byron-Curtiss. "He seemed to be worrying for fear he had not done everything proper. His mind did not lay in coping with romantic situations. He seemed to be truly wracking his brain to think of something that he had forgotten that might trip him up later on."

At last he came to a decision. Lib recalled, "He cleared his throat and asked us, 'Be you women all right?'"

"Yes, we be all right," replied Lib. "What chance have we got to be any other ways?"

Satisfied with what he heard, Atwell slid the key under the door, concluding with these instructions. "Now, Miss Brunson, here's the key. Take it. Indeed I's locked you both in but you says you're fine and you got everything you need. In the morning I'll come and you can give me the key and I'll let you out, and the neighbors can't say but what everything is all right and proper. And besides, you never know what neighbors will say if'n you give them something to talk about."

Lib and her sister were able to keep their date with Wash the next day, and Atwell could congratulate himself that with skill and finesse he had come through the encounter unscathed.

| Recipe | KNOCK-YOUR-SOCKS-OFF BEEF LIVER BRAISED IN WINE |

This meal would have beaten any beef meal
Atwell would have ever tasted.

Ingredients:

1 pound thinly sliced beef liver, cut in serving pieces.

¼ cup flour.

½ teaspoon salt.

⅛ teaspoon pepper.

½ cup chopped onion.

3 tablespoons butter or margarine.

1 can (3 or 4 ounces) sliced mushrooms, drained.

1 beef bouillon cube dissolved in ½ cup boiling water.

½ cup dry red wine.

¼ teaspoon basil.

Directions: Coat liver with mixture of flour, salt and pepper; set aside. Sauté onion in butter until tender. Add liver and brown lightly on both sides. Add mushrooms, bouillon, wine and basil. Cover and simmer 15 minutes or until liver is tender. Makes 4 servings. 🍴

Youthful Tommy O'Hern takes a restful lunch break in the wild-forested foothills of Atwell Martin's Adirondack Country. *Photograph by author*

The Recipes of Ma Getman

MA GETMAN was the owner and operator of the Getman House in Forest-port. Rev. Byron-Curtiss boarded there during 1892-93. "Ma Getman," he remembered, "was a widow and she tried to make her hotel as much like a home as possible. Ma was a square-shooter and an excellent cook. Her services offered no frills but that was made up by her mothering her board-ers. We loved her and never let her down.

"Right from the start, Ma gave me a sound talking to. 'Now look here son,' she said, 'you have been on ice long enough …you're young. You should kick up your heels and prance a bit; the good Lord meant that you should have a little fun now and then, but don't you go rambling around in them woods without you having somebody with you that knows his way around. We like your preaching and we don't want to have you turn up missing at the Sunday services.'"

Charlie O'Conner rented the bar concession at the Getman House. Bryon-Curtiss and O'Conner became good friends. The Reverend said he "initially shied away from the saloon portion of the hotel." In those days, he pointed out, "the local community didn't want their preacher in such places."

Byron-Curtiss tells of Ma Getman's thoughtfulness the day he investi-gated an old cabin for sale. "I was forewarned the building was not much to look at, yet it was placed on a fine piece of land, a wooded site snuggled among the trees. Price: $15 with a quitclaim deed."

"Ma and W. R. Stamburg, my senior warden and as such my right-hand man at Christ Church, said I needed a break from work. All knew of my interest in the lake country. Stamburg and O'Conner volunteered to accompany me to see the North Lake property. After an early breakfast at Getman's, we men, in a heady, cheerful mood, were off with a food basket provided by Ma. She packed ham, sausage, bacon, and salt pork—meats that would stand the long (and non-refrigerated) sixteen-mile trek, and spice up the men's palates and offer a food donation to the table of Cool's Mountain House, where we planned to board that night." In addition to the prepared meats, they also carried "a loaf of bread, fresh eggs packed in corn meal and several dozen crispy fried donuts."

The men stopped at Mulchy Spring for lunch, where they ate Ma's fruit bread. Her recipe evidently sparked The Reverend's interest, because it was found in his camp cookbook.

Byron-Curtiss said of Ma, "She gave generously of her modest means to the church and she had the Ladies' Aid meet frequently in the parlor of the hotel, where she served a generous luncheon." The Reverend was always the recipient of any leftovers.

In addition to Ma's generosity and home-cooking, Byron-Curtiss acknowledged his second love was Ma's beautiful daughter. "I fell head-over-heels

The Getman Hotel, Forestport, N.Y. *Courtesy Leola Schmelzle*

Charley O'Conner claimed a man could put on some weight eating Ma Getman's cooking. *Courtesy Dorothy Mooney*

under her influence. I was so serious that I talked over the prospects of marriage with Ma. She took the more sensible attitude, assuring me that my romantic feeling would pass. She knew I intended to leave Forestport to pursue advance work. She was right, but we remained friends the rest of our lives."

Recipe | **MA'S BLUEBERRY BREAD**

Ingredients:

3 cups flour.

1 cup sugar.

1 tablespoon baking powder.

½ teaspoon salt.

¼ teaspoon baking soda.

1 egg.

1⅔ cup milk.

¼ cup oil (This is substituted from the recipe found in Byron-Curtiss's cookbook).

1 cup blueberries.

¾ cup walnuts (optional).

Directions: Mix everything together and bake at 350°F. for 60 minutes (or until done).

| Recipe | **WOODMAN'S BLUEBERRY STEW** |

Slim Murdock, who also appreciated good cooking, and did quite a bit of it at Otter Brook Camp, offered this unusual recipe in a conversation with me as we drove into the Adirondacks.

"Boil blueberries up with water and a little sugar; then when they're getting soft drop in a few spoonfuls of moist dough made by mixing some of your pancake flour with a little milk or water. Then, by jingo, you will have some blueberry dumplings that you'll always remember. 'Course you can do the same with almost all the other kinds of edible berries that grow wild. Blackberries are especially great that way." —Slim Murdock

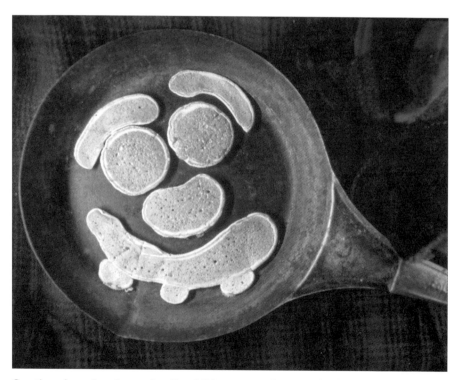

Creating clown-faced pancakes for children was a clever method of baking I learned from Winfred "Slim" Murdock. *Photograph by author*

CHAPTER 20

Cold River-Style Corn Chowder and Hermit Corn Bread

RICHARD SMITH has talked many times about eating Noah John Rondeau's celebrated Everlasting Stew prepared in the same big black iron kettle he used to whip up bear bait. The pot continuously simmered over an open fire that burned inside his cooking wigwam. In it would be a combination of wild and store-bought ingredients. The nearest grocery store was not within a day's hike so it was necessary to learn to make do with what edible ingredients were available.

When I asked Richard what he remembered would have been tossed into the pot he answered, "Let your imagination run wild. Noah wasn't choosy."

Smith continued: "I remember the first time I took a ladle of thick stew. I gathered the mixture was from a new batch of stock because of the chunks of tomatoes. I'd heard his stew pot had a reputation. Everlasting Stew was just that. [A stew Noah continued to add new ingredients to week after week, month after month.]

"The kettle simmered day and night. The stew was there for anyone to take whenever they were hungry. He was a great believer in lentils, barley, beans, rice—bulk ingredients—but also added to the pot the contents of any canned goods a hiker might have left at camp and condiments and chunks of venison, bear, rabbit, hedgehog, beaver, muskrat, squirrel, partridge—actually any kind of meat that might wander his way."

The stew had all to do with survival. Consider that along about the middle of February the broth became kind of thin. Rationing was then in

Noah and Richard Smith, May 17, 1939. *Photograph by Phil McCalvin. Courtesy Helen McCalvin Sawatzki*

order. But all in all, Noah ate as well as a lot of people, maybe even better because the meat market at Cold River was generously stocked and open to him until the late 1940s when his eyesight became less sharp and his age and physical ability made it more difficult for him to hunt.

Smith describes, "I always ate with great relish. Noah and I have dined on sourdough pancakes, corn bread, cuts of bear, every animal we trapped or hunted." Meals were interesting and usually washed down with great mugs of Beech Nut coffee.

I have often wondered what Richard's reaction would have been had I told him about how well my teenage daughter Susie thought she was going to eat over a backpacking trip we planned that was to trace Noah and his regular route from Cold River Hill to Rondeau's high pond and then through Ouluska Pass. Her choice of trail food for the outing—a huge bag of cinnamon balls and pretzels. "Enough for three days," she proudly announced when I inspected the contents of her food bag before we left.[7]

Smith prepared the following recipes for years in his own Handsome Hill cabin along River Road in Lake Placid, New York.

COLD RIVER-STYLE CORN CHOWDER

Ingredients:

4 slices of bacon.

1 medium onion, sliced thin.

2 cups water.

2 cups diced potatoes.

Salt & pepper.

2 cups cream-style corn.

2 cups milk (Smith used whole milk).

1 tablespoon butter.

Directions: Cook bacon until half done. Add onions and cook until bacon and onions are crisp. Drain bacon and onions on paper towels. Crumble the bacon. Put two cups of water and two cups diced potatoes in pan. Add salt and pepper. Simmer about 20 minutes. Add two cups corn and two cups of milk. Simmer 5 minutes. Just before serving add 1 tablespoon butter and the bacon bits. Serves 6–8 people.

HERMIT CORN BREAD. *Corn bread "muffins" as Noah referred to them were standard fare at Cold River during the colder months.*

The hermit cooked over a "kitchen range" that was an old 55-gallon oil drum cut in half lengthwise with a flat heavy steel top as a cooking surface. In the beginning, Noah's "oven" was nothing more than old food cans. He would pour the batter into the 303[8] containers. He had collected enough different sizes of cans for his makeshift ovens to bake several tin-sized loaves for several people if they happened to be in camp. To retain the heat, he placed an inverted larger can over the open top of the smaller can. Next, he placed an even larger can over the two smaller cans. The larger can that covered the two smaller ones captured the heat from the stove top and baked the contents perfectly. The only drawback was he could only produce a few loaves at a time. Of course, if there were many at camp, after the first cans were unloaded they would be re-greased, refilled and were ready to be eaten by the time the first batch was consumed. It took time, but time was plentiful at camp.

After 1943, Noah used a reflector oven. It was given to him by Dr. C. V. Latimer Sr. Noah referred to it as his "Ace Woodsman" because Doc Latimer had punched that name into the metal top with a nail and hammer before presenting the stove as a gift.

Noah enjoyed the small stove-top oven. He baked sourdough biscuits and potatoes in it the first evening. The small heat indicator in the door never failed to steam over on the outside. When they joined forces during the trapping season, Noah told Smith it was his job to wipe the condensation away with a cloth so the rising dial could be watched. "The breadstuffs Noah baked," Smith remembered, "were perfect complements to our meals. I always packed in jars of jams and jellies. The sweetness tasted especially good back there in the woods."

In Smith's later years Richard always used the Quaker® brand yellow corn meal recipe listed below.

Recipe	**CORN BREAD** (Quaker® Yellow Corn Meal Brand)

1¼ cups all-purpose flour.

¾ cup corn meal.

¼ cup sugar.

2 teaspoons baking powder.

½ teaspoon salt (optional).

1 cup skim milk.

¼ cup vegetable oil.

2 egg whites or 1 egg, beaten.

Directions: Heat oven to 400°F. Grease 8 or 9 inch pan. Combine dry ingredients. Stir in milk, oil and egg, mixing just until dry ingredients are moistened. Pour batter into prepared pan. Bake 20–25 minutes or until light golden brown and wooden pick inserted in center comes out clean. Serve warm. 9 servings.

Old-timers fixed corn meal with salt and hot water or milk, often adding maple syrup, honey or sugar to sweeten the mix. The blend was then fried in a greased skillet. Johnny Cake provided a filling meal in the bush. Southerners call it Hoecake.

In 1952, when Marjorie L. Porter interviewed Adirondack native Abram Kilburn from Wilmington, he related a curious true story involving Johnny Cake.

Ira Keese lived his adult life in the mountainous Wilmington region. Ira made his living going around much like old time tinkers. He was a poor man. He lived with families he found employment with and made a living by hiring out his services. Abram Kilburn remembers Ira chopped wood and "did sapping" [worked in the maple sugar bush] in the spring. When he got so old and sickly that he couldn't work and take care of himself, Abram took him in and cared for the sickening man.

"One day," Abram said, "Ira wanted Johnny Cake. I said, "Yes, I can make that. So, I went and mixed some up and he et it and you know within an hour he was dead."

Ira said he went to Wilmington to get some help, telling whoever he called on that his Johnny Cake had killed old Ira, "so I want you to come

Noah's outdoor kitchen table. *Courtesy Richard J. Smith*

up and help me box him up." Abram pointed out that in those days "if you could get a casket at all they'd only be five and a half feet long." Ira was six feet six inches tall. "So," Abram continued, "Ira's feet stuck out over the end of the casket by twelve inches!"

The men talked about what they could do. One fellow told Abram to go get him a hand saw. He pulled the legs up over the casket and sawed them off," putting the remaining parts into the box. The teller emphasized to Marjorie that this was a true story. And, just to prove it he listed off the other men who were there that witnessed the bizarre event. 🍺

Waking up from a comfortable night's rest on Cold River Hill to the smell of breakfast cooking was a joy for Bette O'Hern. *Photograph by author*

CHAPTER 21

A Wigwam Kitchenette and Rascally Raccoons

Recipe **MRS. RONDEAU'S CORN FRITTERS**

Ingredients:

1 cup creamed corn.

1 egg (beaten).

2 rounded tablespoons flour.

2 rounded tablespoons baking powder.

Pinch of salt.

Directions: To egg add corn then sift dry ingredients into mixture. Stir and mix. Fry as you would pancakes. Serve with maple syrup.

★ ★ ★

THERE NEVER WAS a Mrs. Rondeau at Cold River Hill—just a wigwam Noah had named "Mrs. Rondeau's Kitchenette." There were, however, many meals consisting of Daisy Ham and corn fritters. Noah fried fritters in bear grease and bacon fat. It's not recommended.

Adirondack hermit Noah John Rondeau was asked if he had ever tried to grow sweet corn in his vegetable garden. He replied he had, once. The tall surrounding trees allowed precious little sun except in the center of the camp's clearing. His vision of a bountiful harvest never materialized. He joked, "The crop was so stunted I had to get down on my knees to see the ears and besides the deer mice only had to stand on their tiptoes to feast on a banquet of corn-on-the-cob Cold River style."

Never again did he try to grow corn in his vegetable garden. He had enough trouble dealing with the resident "masked bandits"—the raccoons.

Daisy was a brand of canned ham Noah bought at the grocery stores. It was a pressed ham roll, boneless and compact. Noah referred to them as "little gems," while Richard Smith called them "pork rolls of joy."

Noah said, "When sliced and fried the canned ham was delicious; it also produced an abundance of grease that was excellent for frying eggs."

According to Richard Smith, Noah always saved any meat fat as a flavoring for Slam Bang Stew. He said, "The pork rolls of joy eliminated the need to use Crisco, bear grease or bacon grease for frying. The label showed several colorful pigs drawn in a ballet pose." Smith continued, "The product label occasionally provoked Noah to make an amusing comment about the animals dancing on their tiptoes around the label. Simple entertainment to be sure, but we never lacked for humor."

Applying what he learned from Noah, Smith began carrying at least one four-pound Daisy Ham into Noah's camp. Smith explained he willingly packed the weight.

"It was worth its weight in gold," he said. "After I opened a can of the prized ham on the day of my arrival, I sliced off a tiny portion to eat and to use for a bit of cooking grease and flavoring. The remainder I placed in an empty garbage can Noah kept in his Pyramid of Giza wigwam. I carefully wired the top securely to the two handles and then suspended the can from a chain that hung from the inside the wigwam. I remembered some of Noah's comments about raccoons that boldly robbed him of some prime food. I was not about to retire without first making sure my ham was both fool-and-'coon proof if either were around.

"Unfortunately there was one of each that night. With the stealth of a cat burglar, a raccoon jumped up on the can and worked the wired cover loose, making off with my prized ham.

"I awakened the next morning hungry as a bear fresh out of hibernation and ready for a breakfast of ham and eggs. Such a backwoods feast would make my morning repast one to remember. Following the snow path I had brushed out to the wigwam, I entered the interior and discovered to my great dismay

The interior of a cone-shaped woodpile served as Mrs. Rondeau's Kitchenette. Cold River Hill has continued to draw backpackers who look forward to visiting the site of Rondeau's hermitage. *Courtesy Richard J. Smith*

Bill Frenette reported seeing raccoon tracks during an early spring snowshoe to Rondeau's digs at Cold River Hill. Cold River Hill has continued to draw backpackers who look forward to visiting the site of Rondeau's hermitage. *Courtesy Bill Frenette*

Spring Trout & Strawberry Pancakes: Borrowed Tales, Quirky Cures, Camp Recipes

Tom O'Hern, Lt., studies the distant Cold River Country during a November High Peaks climb snack break. *Photograph by author*

the untimely disappearance of my prize foodstuff. All that remained as evidence that a Daisy Ham had ever existed was the calling card Mr. Coon left inside the can.

I was furious but accepted my loss begrudgingly, then immediately planned my revenge. I set a series of No. 4 traps in strategic locations and waited for the bandit to return, as I knew he would. Two nights later he returned to the scene of his crime, still with a well-greased mustache. Try as he did to look innocent, all signs pointed to his guilt.

"After dispatching the raccoon, I reprimanded him about tampering with MY provisions in my sternest voice. Once I had vented myself I condemned him to be skinned to the bone. In the course of two weeks following the incident, I used the bandit's grease to fry all my pan vittles in and I ate his carcass with relish.

Later in the spring following ice-out, I returned to fish Cold River with Noah. After I told him about the local raid he asked how the raccoon tasted. With complete honesty I reported the meat was just like Daisy Ham!"

Pop Baker's Guardian Snake

WINFRED "SLIM" MURDOCK, in his youthful days, worked as a packer and sometimes as a guide for his uncle, Gerald Kenwell. Kenwell maintained a sportsmen's camp along Otter Brook in the Moose River Plains. In Slim's later years, we talked at great length about his connections with the guides he knew and knew about.

When Slim was in his mid-eighties, he made up his mind he'd take one final trip back to see the remains of his Uncle Gerald's camp. I accompanied him.

Throughout our hike, Slim relived various experiences and adventures he'd had packing throughout the 1920s and early '30s. Slim said he learned the following story from his uncle, who heard it from "Pop" Baker.

Frank Baker was a noted guide for the Adirondack League Club. In Frank's later years he took on the surname "Pop." For many years "Pop" was the caretaker of Camp Nit, a camp on Beaver Lake that Gerald's father, Wellington, built in 1895 for a Rochester-based car-wheel tycoon named Harry Chapin.

Pop "fancied himself a good cook in his own right," Slim said with authority. I knew Slim to be an excellent cook, and he wouldn't bestow laurels on anyone if he didn't know it to be so.

Unlike Slim, however, Pop could be a bit cranky if his food wasn't eaten with appreciation. The story is told as Slim related it to me:

> *One day Old Pop drew a group of women who were all on a diet. He made his famous flapjacks, flipping them in the approved fashion, and served platefuls piping hot.*

He sat and watched the women barely nibbling and became highly insulted watching them make such a fuss over them. Deciding something drastic had to be done, he grabbed his rifle and pointed it square at the women. Looking them straight in the eyes, he demanded they *eat every damn crumb of them damn panyeecakes or I'll blow yer brains out.*

Needless to say, the women were terrified and dove into the towering stacks of 'cakes.

Frank "Pop" Baker outside Camp Nit. *Courtesy Margaret Wilcox (The Camp Nit Collection)*

Winfred "Slim" Murdock, circa 1929. *Courtesy Winfred Murdock*

It was customary for camp owners in the Plains to help each other out. Slim and Pop got together whenever Slim packed supplies into Beaver Lake on his way to his uncle's place.

When Harry Chapin sold Camp Nit to Alan and Margaret Wilcox, a former camp guest of Chapin's continued to visit the Inlet-Eagle Bay area and told Margaret with a smile, "You haven't eaten until you've tasted Pop's biscuits."

According to Margaret, the woman was referring to an incident that had happened at Camp Nit years earlier. During an evening meal, someone had remarked how unique his biscuits were compared to what they had eaten. Thinking the enquirer would like to learn his secret, Pop had begun to reveal it was heavy cream, when the woman interrupted, remarking, "Pop, that was a stroke of inspiration to use caraway seeds."

"My God!" Pop shot back in shock. He dashed to the kitchen, lifted the lid of the flour barrel and shouted in disgust, "Just as I suspected! Those damn mice have been at that flour again." After that, he kept a pet snake in the flour barrel.

And that IS the truth, Margaret confirmed.

★ ★ ★

FOLLOWING OUR HIKE to the ruins of Otter Brook Camp, Slim gave me many pictures of Gerald Kenwell's place. One thought-provoking snapshot shows Gerald hanging wet socks from a drying rack that was suspended directly above the wood stove he cooked on. Slim said it wasn't all that unusual for either a sock or a length of long ash from Gerald's ever-present cigarette to drop into the pancake batter or stew he was cooking.

Slim and Gerald maintained a small vegetable garden and liked to grow and use as many fresh vegetables as they could. Contemporary adaptations of recipes using the vegetables they grew follow.

| Recipe | MARIE'S CAMPGROUND ZUCCHINI AND SAUSAGE STEW |

1 lb. loose sausage, cooked and drained and set aside.

1–2 tablespoons olive or vegetable oil.

1 clove garlic, minced (optional).

1 zucchini cut into cubes.

1 large green pepper cubed.

1 onion sliced.

1 can pitted black olives (optional).

1 cup marinara sauce or 1 can stewed tomatoes.

¼ cup grated parmesan cheese.

8 ounce mozzarella cubed (or small pkg.).

1 package (9 ounce) medium pasta shells or other pasta

Directions: Put oil in pan with 1 clove garlic. Dump in all but the sausage, cheeses and marinara or tomatoes. Cook until vegetables are cooked. Add the grated cheese and sausage. Add marinara sauce. Boil medium shells (or any pasta you want). Add shells and stir in mozzarella.

Recipe | **BETTE'S COUNTRY SKILLET GARDEN MEDLEY**

Ingredients:

Combine a variety of optional garden or market vegetables: zucchini, carrots, onions, peppers, green beans, summer squash, onion, garlic, tomatoes, etc.).

Chop or slice vegetables in medium "chunk" sizes…not too fine.

Cook a pound or half a pound of bacon (depending on quantity of vegetables you are using). Remove bacon, drain skillet, crumble bacon when cool.

Add a few tablespoons of olive oil (depending on size of skillet and quantity of vegetables) to the skillet.

Sauté vegetables until desired softness or firmness. Add your choices of spices and herbs.

This recipe can vary each time it's made. Be creative and enjoy! 🐟

Opposite: Gerald Kenwell preparing biscuits at Otter Brook Camp. Slim said a bit of cigarette ash in the mix never dampened anyone's appetite. Circa 1940. *Courtesy Ora Kenwell*

CHAPTER 23

Adirondack Mosquitoes and Pop Baker's Specialty

IN THE ADIRONDACKS, swarms of stinging, biting, crawling and flying insects abound from spring into late summer. Natives throughout the Adirondack Park have a multitude of stories about the insects, about the concoctions they brewed up as repellent, and about the unsuspecting vacationers.

One old-time fly-dope mixture called for 3 parts Pine Tar, 2 parts Castor Oil, 1 part Penny oil. It was to be mixed and heated slowly to blend.

Caroline Nelson was one such person with strong camping ties to the central Adirondacks. Her family had owned a camp in Eagle Bay for over a generation. "I have great memories about the lake country and of my grandfather's guiding," she began before launching into a favorite horseback trip she took with her friend Emily Chapin in the 1920s.

ON A TRIP into beaver-shaped-tail mile-long Beaver Lake deep in the heart of the Moose River Plains, Caroline met "Pop" Baker. Pop, a caretaker at Camp Nit, had been a guide in his younger years and had developed a reputation as an excellent cook and an amusing host among the visitors who would walk or horseback to Beaver Lake to fish or just pay a neighborly visit to the old-timer.

Camp Nit was Emily's family wilderness camp.

Carolyn recalled that as the first faint shadows of twilight began to fall across the lake, Emily and she were seated with Pop on the high deck, which was constructed so the viewing platform extended out over the lake. The girls were rehashing the day's activity.

"I remember Pop served us warm slices of banana bread and tea," she recalled. "At a point in our conversation he interrupted to point out some activity; handing us binoculars to pass around. Across the lake, a black bear cub was busily scooping ants from a rotted log split open by its mother. In the bay nearly covered with lily pads, two deer were extracting roots and succulent grasses. All was serenely quiet; only the gentle lapping of water kicked up by a mild breeze broke the silence."

As the group sat taking in the wild setting, Pop cautioned that with night would come mosquitoes. The girls had been on many wilderness trips. They were aware of mosquitoes. The insects weren't something to be concerned with other than the buzzing annoyance and bites. They had, however, been forewarned about bears and all knew the dangers that could accompany a horse's fear of bears if the animal was frightened.

Beaver Lake circa 1905. *Courtesy Margaret Wilcox (The Camp Nit Collection)*

Carolyn and Emily took in the wild scene from the high deck overlooking Beaver Lake.
Courtesy Margaret Wilcox (The Camp Nit Collection)

Pop agreed with them. An injury could happen if a frightened horse bucked in even a not-too-spirited way. That put aside, he warned that earlier in the week the insects had been acting up, tormenting the deer until they drove them crazy. The girls just laughed and told Pop they would not be put off by a few mosquitoes.

Pop said a visitor had told him the same thing just last week. The man had sat unconcerned right there until he heard an ominous drone of startling magnitude. The buzz emanated from the stagnant swamp water on the opposite side of camp. Looking up, the man saw a rapidly approaching dark object that quickly became recognizable as a formation of two titan mosquitoes descending toward him.

As fast as was humanly possible, Pop turned toward the camp door at a dead run. He knew he needed to get inside quickly before he was spotted.

His guest, unfortunately, was too late; the mosquitoes had seen him. His only chance, however slim, was to leap as if his life depended on it into the lake.

Mr. Guest hurtled the railing hardly a whisker ahead of the blood-thirsty insects. But before he was able to drop like a cannon ball into the depths, he was lifted straight up in the air and carried out over the water by the mosquitoes.

In his totally aghast state, he thought he could hear his two captors arguing over his elimination. "Want to eat him on the opposite bank or in the backwater?" he heard one ask the other. The replying voice said, "Are you crazy? We had better take him deeper into the woods before the big ones come along and take him away from us."

Terrified and thinking he was close to death, the man flailed out at the mosquitoes with his arms and furiously kicked his legs until they lost their grip and dropped him into Beaver Lake. The waves carried him toward shore, where he was pulled out by Pop. The camp guest left the Moose River Plains the next morning, swearing never to return for another vacation in the Adirondacks.

As for Carolyn and her friend, they escaped the sad fate of Pop's earlier visitor. Their wilderness trip to Beaver Lake and Pop's knack of storytelling was a happy part of their camping tradition.

| Recipe | FRANK "POP" BAKER'S BANANA BREAD |

Ingredients:
3 over-ripe bananas mashed and whipped.
½ cup sugar.
2 eggs.
½ cup butter.
2 cups flour.
1 teaspoon baking soda.
¼ cup chopped walnuts (optional).
Directions: mix together the mashed bananas, sugar, eggs and butter. Add to that mixture the flour, soda and nuts. Lightly grease one bread pan. Bake at 350°F. for 50 to 60 minutes. Cool before slicing. 🍶

A welcoming campfire meal. Pharoah Lake Wilderness Area in the eastern Adirondack. Circa 1930s. *Courtesy Special Collections, Feinberg Library, SUNY College at Plattsburgh*

SECTION FOUR

Treasury of Timeless Tales and Trail-tested Recipes

HEREIN ARE SOME time-honored recipes, boisterous tales and down-to-earth experiences of natives and backpackers, anglers and cooks, vacationers and camp owners.

There were days when my entertainment at camp consisted of reading and rocking under a covered porch, packing a picnic lunch in my kayak and taking off for a leisurely paddle, bushwhacking in search of the once-known site of a far-off cabin, and enjoying the stillness of a colorful autumn day as I leisurely walked a forest path. Often I hoped I would never have to leave the laid-back routine of peaceful mountain living. A favorite drink or stock recipe can couple me in spirit to the mountains.

The camp porch is a refuge from hot interiors and the uncontrollable outdoor weather. A comfortable quarters for relaxing in the shade, eating and sleeping, reading and peaceful gazing. *Courtesy Helen Menz*

CHAPTER 24

Raccoons Loved Berry Brandy

ANNA AND CHARLEY BROWN'S camp was once home to Kettle Jones. Kettle was a well-known trapper and producer of hand-split cedar shingles back in the 1880s and '90s. Toward the end of the 19th century Kettle's strenuous days were over. Old age found him doing more custom woodworking, gardening and cooking.

Kettle's place was a small log cabin in a clearing approximately a mile upstream from the foot of North Lake in the vicinity of Sugarloaf Mountain. His beds of rhubarb and asparagus were astonishingly productive.

There was no end to what Kettle could do. He had a knack with a drawshave. Kettle whittled and fitted all kinds of tools that required wooden handles. He told stories and even foretold the future by reading tea leaves.

But his specialty product was wild berry brandy brewed in a homemade still. Gossip had it that Kettle was willing to extract teeth and deliver babies after downing two glasses of his wild berry brandy. He cooked the concoction in a large black iron kettle that hung from a crane over the outdoor fireplace. Those who drank it reported the Adirondack wild berry brew restored inflamed joints. Kettle sold his herbal medicine in pint glass fruit jars. He claimed it was "suitable for man, woman, or beast."

Kettle had two pet raccoons. The animals were his drinking and business partners. Both man and animal were reported to dribble the brandy as a dressing on all the food they consumed. The raccoons always ate from plates and sat at the table with Kettle. Many besotted customers who were on "The Juice" were taken with the antics of his brandy-loving pets. Kettle sold his beloved pets over and over, having trained the animals to open the latch to the cage and escape, arriving back home before the customer ever made the final bend around Atwell Bay. According to those who knew Kettle, "The ruse worked every time."

Rev. Byron-Curtiss reported that he directed a group of young clergymen to Kettle's. They were freshly graduated from the seminary and had come to his camp for a vacation. "What a hoot they got themselves in," reported the holy man as he related the story at what was billed as the Great Event of North Lake—Anna and Charley Brown's silver anniversary on September 6, 1930. "Those fresh-behind-the-ears graduates ended up drinking side by side with Kettle and the raccoons!"

Recipe | **COLD SPRING THIRST QUENCHER**

This drink will revive the most wilted summer-time camp guest.
Ingredients:
1 cup orange juice.
1 cup unsweetened pineapple juice.
¼ cup lemon juice.
¼ cup maraschino cherry juice.
1 cup dry ginger ale.
2 tablespoons honey.
1 pint vanilla ice cream.
2 tablespoons sliced maraschino cherries.
Directions: Mix fruit juices and ginger ale; add honey; mix well.
Chill thoroughly. Add ice cream; stir until blended. Serve in a tall glass; top with a sprinkling of cherry slices. Makes 1½ quarts.

Recipe | **ADIRONDACK LEMONADE**

This triple fruity flavor makes this an extra-special summer-time drink.
It's as cooling as a mountain breeze.
Ingredients:
1 6-ounce can of frozen lemonade concentrate.
1 12-ounce can (1½ cups) of apricot nectar, chilled.
1 12-ounce can (1½ cups) unsweetened pineapple juice, chilled.

1 cup (give or take) of ginger ale, chilled.

Directions: Add 1 can of water to the lemonade concentrate; add fruit juices. Place ice cubes in six 12-ounce glasses. Divide the fruit juice mixture among the glasses. Fill with ginger ale. Trim glasses with lemon slices.

The Party. After a day of baking cakes and rolls, cooking chicken and making home-made potato chips, the party boomed and sang and thought of the fun to come as they lifted their cups in joy.

1. Tina Goodsell Titus; 2. George Goodsell; 3. Gerald Goodsell; 4. Robert Goodsell; 5. Mrs. George Goodsell; 6.?

Cold tea, root beer, ale, buttermilk, and sweet cider were good and refreshing, but the prize drink was the cold, cold water from an Adirondack spring.

Courtesy Town of Webb Historical Association

Campfire girls, winter 1920, trail break. A warm beverage prepared over a fire in a tea pail was a welcome break. *Courtesy Town of Webb Historical Association*

CLERICS' PUNCH

Ingredients:

⅕ quart of ruby port.

⅕ quart of Burgundy.

1 orange.

Whole cloves.

2 cinnamon sticks.

Roast Orange*.

Directions: Combine port and Burgundy in large saucepan. Cut unpeeled orange in ¼-inch slices. Notch peels evenly (at about ¾-inch intervals) to form flowers, stud center of each with whole clove and add to wine with cinnamon. Bring to boil, reduce heat and simmer 30 minutes. Remove cinnamon sticks. Preheat punch 5 hot wine mixture. Add Roast Orange. Serve hot in punch cups. Makes 12 servings.

*ROAST ORANGE: Stud whole orange with whole cloves in attractive pattern; bake on a small piece of aluminum foil in 350°F. oven about 1 hour, or until soft and darkened. 🍸

William Thomas O'Hern and his inseparable "Fishin' Bear" enjoys picnics around an Adirondack fire pit. Summer 2014. *Photograph by author*

CHAPTER 25

Brownie the Camp Dog

It was a warm August early evening, so we had the screen door open. An agreeable supper cooking odor of Bette's meatballs waffled out from the camp as I scrubbed an iron kettle with sand, small gravel, and water at the lakeshore. I had uncovered the antique iron find from a pile of debris at an old Goose Neck Lake lumber camp site. It had layers of burnt grime which were difficult to remove. In the past I have used a wire brush and built a fire and placed old iron ware on a bed of hot coals. This has always burned the grime off but left the cookware very rusty but clean. My sand and water method is slower and more labor intensive but also works well. Once an iron container is cleaned all that is left is to let it thoroughly dry, then season it by generously smearing it with vegetable oil, and place it in a 200-degree oven for a few hours.

Following supper I was thumbing through Rev. Byron-Curtiss' photo album when I came across a 1920 photograph of the former camp owner sitting in the sun with his dog Brownie. The following day I was paddling past the site of Dell Bellinger's South Lake camp. "Brownie the Spaniel" rose from this inspiration and what I knew about the Reverend and Dell.

★ ★ ★

"TALL TALKIN'" at Jerry's North Lake camp has been termed "Parting With the Dog" ever since that celebrated tall-tale session when Dell Bellinger offered a spaniel puppy to the person who could tell the biggest whopper. Well, that evening the stories started rolling and not one teller could tell the truth. The gathering went on clear into the next morning. "If it had not been for Dell and his pet squirrel, I'd might never in a million years have gotten into the story-telling business," Byron-Curtiss would later say of the get-together.

The story that follows is true, Rev. Byron-Curtiss said. He learned it from a few "old saints and sinners who hugged the pot-bellied stove on cold days at Sam Utley's 'Harness Shop Senate.'" However," to protect the privacy of Jerry and Nellie's relatives, last name, location of North Lake camp, and likeness' have been altered," B-C noted, "at the request of relatives."

As her husband finished his last cup of coffee, with Nellie cleaning the mess from the previous night from the table, Jerry broke into a renewed storytelling routine. He was the perfect fall guy for all the camp humorists. But, against Nellie, he had little or no defense. It was obvious Nellie was ready to break up the assembly when she delivered a platter down on his head. CRACK went the china, followed by a WHIZ as a butcher knife barely missed the coffee mug when thrown into the surface of the wooden table with dexterity and spirit as her husband began to pick up the prolonged meeting by declaring, "I've never told a lie the whole night."

Nellie was not interested in hearing one story bigger and harder to believe than the one before.

Rev. Byron-Curtiss and Brownie. *Courtesy Thomas and Doris Kilbourn (The A. L. Byron-Curtiss Collection)*

Now, every man at the table knew he didn't have a chance of winning that pup on account of Jerry's declaration, so Dell proclaimed Jerry the winner but awarded the prize to his wife.

"Nellie, you get the pup," Dell said. And the saints and sinners (who were the majority) all agreed with him.

That pup became Rev. Byron-Curtiss' dog, Brownie. Nellie had no use for the spaniel. "I could have written a weekly gossip column on the social life of the North Lake folks each week for the rest of my life," he volunteered, "and never run out of truth and tales."

When Nellie announced that she would have fritters for supper it whetted Jerry's and The Reverend's appetites, and they waited impatiently for the supper hour.
Courtesy Piseco Historical Society

BLACK RIVER MEATBALLS

Ingredients:

1½ pounds lean ground beef.

½ pound lean ground pork.

½ cup bread crumbs soaked in ¼ cup cream.

2 eggs, beaten.

2 tablespoons minced onion.

¼ teaspoon salt.

Dash of ground pepper.

¼ teaspoon nutmeg.

Directions: Mix all ingredients together and form into meat balls and brown in hot oil. Juice may be thickened with cornstarch and water. Serve in a chafing dish.

CAST IRON SKILLET MEAT-BALL DINNER

Ingredients:

1 pound ground beef.

2 tablespoons chopped onion.

2 tablespoons chopped green pepper.

¼ cup corn meal

1 teaspoon salt.

1½ teaspoons dry mustard.

1 teaspoon chili powder.

½ cup milk.

1 slightly beaten egg.

¼ cup flour.

2 tablespoons fat.

2 cups tomato juice.

3 potatoes, quartered.

6 carrots, halved.

12 to 18 small onions.

Salt.

Directions: Combine meat, onions, green pepper, corn meal, seasonings, milk, and egg; mix thoroughly and form 12 balls. Sprinkle with flour, brown in hot fat. Place in casserole or iron fry pan. To fat in skillet add remaining flour; blend and add tomato juice. Cook thick; pour over meat balls. Arrange vegetables around meat balls. Add salt. Cover. Bake in moderate oven (350°F.) 1 hour. Serves 6.

Recipe **OLD-TIME SAVORY MEAT BALLS**

Ingredients:

2 slices bread.

2 tablespoons water.

1 pound ground beef.

½ pound liver sausage.

1 slightly beaten egg.

3 tablespoons chopped onion.

½ teaspoon salt.

⅛ teaspoon nutmeg.

⅓ cup flour.

3 tablespoons fat.

1 bouillon cube.

½ cup boiling water.

Directions: Soak bread in 2 tablespoons water. Add meats, egg, onion, salt, nutmeg; mix thoroughly. Form into small balls. Roll in flour; brown in hot fat. Dissolve bouillon cube in ½ cup boiling water. Pour over meat balls. Simmer 30 minutes. Makes about 15 meat balls.

Recipe **BROWNIE'S HOME-COOKED DELIGHT**

This is an alternative to commercially-made dog food. It's an old-time home-made recipe with some modern adjustments that uses ingredients that are readily available. It's more labor intensive and more expensive than prepared pet food. Let your dog determine which is their favorite.

Ingredients:

1 pound ground chicken, turkey, or beef.

2 cups brown rice (Barley or oats may be substituted).

5 cups of water (Some people substitute 2 cups broth with 3 cups of water, but it adds to the expense).

1 frozen package of mixed vegetables (fresh is even better). *Directions:* Brown the meat, then add the veggies to the kettle. Vegetables are better if put through a potato ricer. A modern method is to use a food processor. It breaks the vegetables up to release more of the nutrients. Dogs don't chew their food. Next, add the rice and water to the kettle. Bring the mixture to a boil, then reduce the heat and let it simmer for 20–30 minutes.

The rice will be cooked when the liquid is gone. Cool. The formula makes 9-12 cup servings. Form each serving into a ball, place on a cookie sheet and cover. Can be placed in the refrigerator or place in plastic freezer bags and store for later use. 🍴

Dell Bellinger's keen senses felt a chill come over his body as the hair stood up on his arms the way it does before a lightning strike. The tall talking, fast thinking guide knew Nellie met business. *Courtesy Thomas A. Gates*

CHAPTER 26

Camp Ice Houses

BACK AROUND the corner of time, camps had an ice house, a wooden ice-box or both. My grandparent's home and camp had an icebox. They bought blocks of ice from the People's Ice Company and from their camp's hamlet store. Matty delivered the huge blocks in his delivery wagon, which was pulled by a horse. I used to help carry the clear solid blocks that were held tight with ice tongs. I still have the tongs and ice pick with advertising stamped on the wooden handle plugging "Pure-Crystal Clear-Hard Ice. Telephone 2-3161," which was used to chip shaving and to break off smaller blocks when we loaded the ice compartment.

The wooden icebox cooler dated back to the early 1900s. It looked like a wooden cupboard. I believe the wood was white oak. Sometime during the 1950s power came down the road. The cooler had served its purpose for many decades by the time it was replaced with a new electric refrigerator.

A few neighboring camps had their own icehouses. They cut lake ice each winter to fill the building. The structures were designed and built with double walls into which insulation was packed. Sawdust and wood chips, hay, marsh or swamp grass, buckwheat chaff, bark, and charcoal all were used for insulating material. If built correctly and lined properly, an ice house could insulate so well that shrinkage from melting was only about 30%.

Playing inside an icehouse was frowned on for obvious reasons. The ice, meats and liquids kept inside could come to some bad end.

One of the most outstanding kinds of cake I've ever eaten was once kept in grandma's icebox. It's an exceptional dessert—one I always look forward to enjoying.

ICE HOUSE BANANA CAKE

Sift together in a bowl:

2½ cups cake flour.

1⅝cups sugar.

1¼ teaspoons baking powder.

1¼ teaspoons baking soda.

1 teaspoon salt.

Add: ⅔ cup shortening.

⅛ cup buttermilk.

1¼ cups mashed bananas (4).

Add: ⅛ cup buttermilk.

2 large eggs.

Beat 2 minutes.

Add: ¾ cup chopped nuts.

Bake in three 8in. layers at 350°F. for 30-35 minutes

BUTTER FROSTING

Boil and cool ¾ cup milk. Combine with one egg white–beat well. *Add:* 1 cup sugar, ½ cup shortening, ¼ lb. butter, and 1 teaspoon vanilla to milk and egg white. Beat 20 minutes.

SQUIRREL TOP EGG NOG

The day I interviewed Indian Lake resident, Ethel Tripp, she offered me a glass of her homemade egg nog. I had only been familiar with the store-bought variety. Ethel said back in her younger days it was typical to make your own. Ethel's father was Fred "Mossie" Maxium a well-known Raquette Lake Adirondack guide for J. P. Morgan at Camp Uncas, and at Kamp Kill Kare for Lt. Governor Timothy Woodruff. I had recently found the former site of his Squirrel Top camp. Ethel was thrilled something still remained of the place. I regaled her with details of the challenging bush-whack east of Sagamore Lake that day as we drank egg nog. Ethel laughed as she remembered liking the holiday drink so well that as a young girl she would slip into the family's ice house to sip it out of a large blue-speckled crock. That afternoon she sang to me her Squirrel Top song, so I named her parents' recipe in honor of her dad's Adirondack camp.

Ingredients:

½ pt. heavy cream.

1 quart milk.

4 eggs separated.

4 rounding tablespoons sugar.

1 cup white rum.

Directions: Beat yolks and sugar, add rum slowly beating in. Add 1 quart milk, the whipped egg whites and whipped cream. Chill well. 🏺

Ice houses are buildings used to store ice throughout the year, commonly used prior to the invention of the electric and gas refrigerator. Adirondack ice houses were man-made. Blocks of winter ice cut from lakes were stored inside. Many were buildings with various types of insulation.

During the winter, blocks of lake ice and snow would be stored in the ice house and packed with insulation—often sawdust or straw. Ice would remain frozen for many months, often until the following winter. The main function of an ice house was the storage of perishable foods. *Courtesy Town of Webb Historical Association*

George Robitelle, 1941. Homemade ice cutting machine.
Courtesy Town of Webb Historical Association

CHAPTER 27

Bear Banquet

CAMPING ALONE in the Adirondacks can have its pitfalls, as evidenced by my hiking buddy's loss of good sense while on a solo outing in the West Canada Lake Wilderness.

Paul, a veteran of over thirty years of experience, had a night-time surprise. This is how I recall he related it.

"It was a gloomy dark night. Rain had been falling for several hours. Reading by candlelight about 10 p.m. I heard a rustle behind the shelter. I figured it might be an approaching late-evening hiker or just amplified padding of small nocturnal mammals on the forest floor." He didn't concern himself about it other than think it would be nice to have company on a wet dreary night.

Minutes later, his generally stalwart nature gave way when he saw the head of a large black bear turn the corner of the lean-to. The bear rolled its head upward and sideways–sniffing the air. Immediately, it climbed onto the floor and headed directly to Paul's backpack, which was resting against the back wall.

Paul knew it was important to keep food in a bear-proof canister or hang it high between trees but because of the rain he decided to wing it "just that once."

The bear appeared so quickly and unexpectedly, Paul said, "I didn't have any time to react. Before I knew it the bear was in the lean-to. I had no time to yell, blow my whistle or bang on a metal cook pot. If I had I'm sure the loud noise would have scared it off. I was too startled, and besides the bear was so close at that point I was afraid if I startled it, it might have injured me."

Rattled by the bear, Paul's first thought was not to make a sound. By then he'd known that by breaking a cardinal rule he was in for an experience he wouldn't have wished for.

Author's and Paul Sirtoli's winter camp at Gooseneck Lake. No matter the season or weather, food bags need to be strung high. *Author's Photo*

A makeshift snowshoe platform serves as a Gooseneck Lake kitchen stove. A hot beverage and welcome oatmeal provided a warm breakfast feast on an otherwise bitter cold winter morning. *Author's Photo*

"I was lying in my sleeping bag," he recalled. "I quickly pulled the hood over my head and kept still. I could feel the animal's body against my bag as it began tearing at my pack. I figured at that point I needed to stay motionless or run the risk of being stepped or sat on.

"I was so scared. I began to pray. I had probably recited fifteen Hail Marys by the time I fainted"—from fright and the heat inside the bag."

It was about "five the next morning when I woke up. I had a flashlight inside my bag. When I shined it around, I found my pack shredded. All that was left of a three-day supply of food was a half-gnawed orange lying on the ground."

Knowing the gnashed fruit was the only thing to eat during a long, hungry fifteen-mile trek back to his car parked at the trailhead, he ate it.

I kidded him after learning of the experience. I told him he had a Higher Authority on his side, his reward for working at the Vatican when he was younger.

We decided the bear was probably "West Canada Bob," a legendary black bear at the time. Many careless backpackers in the wilderness area had lost food to the food-stealing bruin. During that same year hikers had drawn pictures of Bob and jotted notes about his exploits in almost every lean-to register in the West Canada Wilderness from Brooktrout to Pillsbury Lake.

I reminded my buddy of my oft-repeated warning whenever we made a late-night camp: *Always take the time to hang the food.* He never failed to do it from that day on.

You tell me which centuries-old species has the best instincts: Man or bear?

I thank the Lord bears were created and are present in the Adirondacks. There have been and probably will always be a never-ending flow of stories about the largest mammals that inhabit the Adirondack Mountains. 🐻

CHAPTER 28

Paul's Food for a Three-Day Backpacking Trip

PAUL SIRTOLI reported that as a backpacker he is not "an exotic guy" when it comes to packing food for an extended trip. I'll also toss in that he is, like me, careful about limiting his intake of saturated fats, trans fats and sodium.

Foods have to be lightweight nowadays. In our early days of backpacking we had the habit of meeting on Friday nights at a Howard Johnson's. There were several situated throughout the Adirondacks. We would gorge, taking advantage of the restaurant's all-you-can-eat menu, then sleep in the back of my van. Those nights we consumed three and four platters of fried clams were memorable occasions. I recall that one November night a couple of women who were with us to climb Santanoni Mountain the next morning shouted they couldn't stand the air. Sleeping outside on the ground at the trailhead was far better than staying in a confined van even though we had the windows open.

Today's food supply for a three-day trip relies on more healthy, simple choices. Breakfast is oatmeal with raisins. For lunch there's any combination of granola, a tube of peanut butter and jelly for sandwiches, bread, gorp—a mixture of chocolate candies, seeds, nuts and dried fruits—cheese, peanuts and cheese bars, figs, an apple or orange. Supper is some kind of instant dinner in a package that calls for adding a bit of oil and water to the contents and boiling it. There are other standards, like cans of tuna fish, cookies, crackers, chocolate chips and whatever Paul can mooch off friends. He is also never without garlic cloves which he chews on "for an appetizer at any time of the day" he likes to say.

"If I am looking for a beverage," he says, "I boil fir needles or pine needles. They are rich in vitamin C. As for water, I rely on a filter before drinking water."

Lt. Paul Sirtoli; Rt. David Pisaneschi. Paul continues to bushwhack and share his 45 years of camp knowledge with a new generation of outers. *Author's Photo*

Without a doubt, Paul is frugal. He saves packets of jelly from restaurants and pre-mixes almost everything at home. "I'm opposed to buying the expensive packets," he points out. It's also a better rule because the nutritional content can be controlled. That said, we have sat at trailheads and consumed up to three one-pound packages of Keebler Vanilla Cream cookies before hitting the trail. And why? Paul and I are conflicted. His explanation is, "I generally bring no food specifically for bears, but will always share what I have with them, mostly under duress!!!" To that I add we are both addicted to cookies.

Piseco Lake. Bears were once common attractions at town dumps.
Courtesy Piseco Historical Society

CHAPTER 29

Wilderness Foods and Trail Recipes

WITH THE CONVENIENCE of a seemingly endless array of grocery items that can be purchased at a super store today, the following wilderness recipes are outdated. Just the same, they offer a feel of what campers of an earlier era prepared to drink and eat when camping.

Recipe | **WOODSMAN'S COFFEE**

To each cup of water add one tablespoon of coffee. Use cold water. Place over the fire and let come to a boil. Set pot where it will remain hot, almost at a boil, for five to ten minutes.

Recipe | **CAMPERS HASHED BROWN POTATOES**

To five or six medium-sized boiled potatoes, sliced, add three tablespoons of pork or bacon fat or melted butter. Place in a skillet and fry slowly until the potatoes are well heated. Now cook a little faster for about one minute. With a table knife press the potatoes down firmly. Try them by lifting up a bit at the edge. If they are brown, place a plate over the skillet. Now with a holder place your hand on the plate and hold it firmly and turn the skillet upside down and the browned potatoes will be on the plate ready for the table, brown side up.

With proper planning, a backpacker can carry a well-stocked "pantry" in their backpack. Here, the author sleds his gear and an antique sink across Bear Pond during the winter as he began to salvage the contents from Bear Pond camp. *Author's Photo*

LAZY BREAD

Ingredients:

2 cups flour.

1 teaspoon salt.

Milk or water.

1 teaspoon baking soda.

2 teaspoons cream of tartar.

2 tablespoons melted lard.

Directions: Sift dry ingredients and add enough milk or water to make a soft batter. Have batter soft enough to beat with a spoon. Add melted lard to the batter before starting to beat it. Pour into a greased bake tin and bake in a hot oven.

TROUT CHOWDER

Pare and dice two or three potatoes of good size and place in a boiling pot. Cover with water and cook slowly until about half done. Place trout separately in boiling water—enough to cover them—and let them boil for five minutes to remove the meat from the bones. Put the trout meat back in the water you used to boil it; add one-half can corn, one can evaporated milk, the half cooked potatoes, one-quarter pound butter, salt and pepper, and place back on the fire. Cook slowly for ten minutes and serve. (Onions add to the flavor of the chowder.)

CAMPFIRE COCOA

To four rounded tablespoons of cocoa add one-half cup of sugar. Add milk enough to make a paste. Beat this until it is smooth. To one can of evaporated milk add one quart boiling water; add the cocoa paste, stir thoroughly and let come to a boil. Less water and more milk will make it richer. 🍸

Camp Sheldon. An Adirondack tent camp made a happy comfortable summertime hangout. Meat and vegetable kebabs served up a unique, yummy food.
Courtesy Piseco Historical Society

CHAPTER 30

Fishing Horn Lake and Traditional Camp Meals

APPROXIMATELY ELEVEN MILES northeast from the head of North Lake in Township 5 lies Horn Lake. It was, and still is, a mecca for fishermen willing to bushwhack. A strong back is a prerequisite. More than a hundred years ago, city sports hired guides, for they invariably needed to "lug out a whacking big mess of trout," according to letters Ralph Merritt wrote describing his many treks to the remote trouty body of water.

Reading Merritt's letters written between 1893–1906 and hearing recent claims that Horn's "a natural hatchery," and "all you need to do is locate the three springs, then sprinkle whole-kernel corn and oatmeal and wait for the trout to bite," I naturally was spurred to try my hand. Horn Lake lived up to its reputation. Angling there is fantastic. Reaching the lake is also a bit of a challenge.

Horn Lake is one of the highest major bodies of water in the Moose River (South Branch) watershed. Most of the water is less than twenty feet deep, although the shore drops off rather abruptly into ten feet of water. A pocket of deeper water lies along the west shoreline in front of the former location of the old Horn Lake Camp.

Surface vegetation is negligible, but the shallower portions of the bottom support a good growth of bladderwort. Most of the shoreline is sand, gravel or rocks, more or less overlaid by a thin layer of sediments in most areas.

The aesthetic shoreline makes it enough of a destination, but for those anglers who want to wet a line, Horn has enjoyed the reputation of being a consistent producer of trout.

On one fishing expedition I sat on opposite ends in an old aluminum boat someone dragged in, probably over the snow. My buddy and I faced each other. We anchored at a wooden stake that marks the location of one spring hole and began to pull in fish. Strikes came so often we became giddy. Catches of 14 to 16-inch fish were occasionally made. A system quickly evolved that reminded me of a comment Merritt had made in one of his letters. "When I hooked a trout I simply thrust the tip of my rod over to my partner who next drew in the line hand-over-hand, unhooked the trout, readjusted the lure and tossed it back into the water. When he hooked one, I did the same with his catch." The only difference was we caught-and-released.

A portion of Merritt's spring 1906 fishing trip follows. Rev. Byron-Curtiss was his fishing buddy on this trip. The Reverend tells of his memory of Merritt.

"My first opportunity to venture to Horn came about because of an accident to Ralph Merritt, a camp guest, during the later days of spring, 1906. Ralph was a well-to-do Roman, a member of my congregation and an individual who rode a hobby for all it was worth. He was also generous. The first season he came to camp he insisted on buying all the supplies and he hired a team to drive us from the Buffalo Head train station to the head of North Lake. Once in camp he noted the absence of human comforts and promised on his return more furnishings would be forthcoming so as, 'to make the little place more comfortable.' The one feature of camp life he did not care for was the deer mice, and there were plenty. The following spring he donated four iron bedsteads with hair mattresses. Included, too, was a power skiff, the first motor boat ever on the lake.

"Poor Merritt. He did have some shortcomings. One was the image he had developed at his Rome club. He had a reputation as a mighty fisherman. When he announced he was off to North Lake on a fishing adventure he also boasted that he would return with enough fish to throw a trout supper for the club. The bluster was sincere and it might have been met had it not been for his tender city feet. Upon Merritt's arrival he laced on his newly purchased mountain boots, a nice piece of leather had they been broken in. Following a few short hiking and fishing trips wearing these boots, his heels became badly blistered. There was indeed physical pain, but the greatest distress came from his psychological disappointment and despair. He whined and whined, 'What am I to do, Reverend? I have a reputation to uphold.' Over breakfast one morning he once again renewed his whining and bemoaned his bad luck. I knew he would be departing shortly. Wanting to help, I was struck with a brilliant idea. 'Tell you what, Ralph,' I began. 'If you will hire a guide to accompany me, I'll go to Horn Lake and bring you out a pack basket of trout.'

"Sore feet or not, old Merritt jumped off his chair and danced a short jig in his bare feet as he exclaimed, 'That's the stuff. Let's get down to the foot of the lake right now and hire a guide right away.' I will own up that my readiness to make the long trip to Horn was more for the adventure farther into the wilderness and the fun I would get out of it than it was by any sympathy for him and his smarting heels.

North Star Camp, Horn Lake, Circa 1890s. *Courtesy Bert Sperry*

and The Adirondack Characters Who Cooked Them Up   179

Fishing and picnics with all the trimmings go hand-in-hand. Lt. standing: Aunt Neelie, Uncle Amos. Lt. seated: Richard Downs, Edward T. Downs, Annie Prescott. Rt. Mary Louise Prescott Downs (aka Aunt Min), Edwin A. Prescott (Edwin is holding baby Maud.) *Courtesy Special Collections, Feinberg Library, SUNY College at Plattsburgh*

"Later that day we rowed to the foot and began to make inquiries. Of the twenty-five or thirty individuals there, eight were males of the younger variety. We found one available man, named Smith, sort of a handyman at George Crandall's cottage. He was a rather taciturn person and showed little enthusiasm. No, he had never been to Horn Lake. Yet he wasn't completely uninterested in the proposal. He named his charge per day and emphasized he knew all about camping, yet he would not undertake to cook the meals.

"I had suggested a guide because I did not feel it prudent to plunge alone into a region unknown to me. Merritt agreed to pay, so we passed over the man's inexperience and limitations. In the aftermath of more parleying over the fee, Smith agreed to be at my camp by seven o'clock the next morning.

"Before the mist of early morning had ceased to hang over the placid waters, Smith and I were off. Few first trips ever excited me more than the promise this one held for me. We carried the usual duffel in our pack baskets: blankets, bread, coffee, frying pan, tin cups and plates, an axe and so forth. I made a mistake by including cans of tinned food such as tomatoes, beans, green peas and corn. I never made that mistake again. I learned that the weight of a load grows heavy on a long overland journey. In all my remaining years spent on the trail I was content to put up with dehydrated food, the only exception being a small can of evaporated milk. I was going to go light or in the words of Yankee Calvin Coolidge, 'Go without.'"

Recipe | **DEHYDRATED VEGETABLES AND POWDERED FOOD**

Dried veggies and powdered food were available and carried by backpackers during the 1930s. Some of the light convenience camp supplies of the day were spinach, potatoes, carrots, cabbage, beans, and turnips, along with soup powders: tomato, bean, oxtail, and mock turtle. There were also powdered eggs and milk. All were to be reconstituted with water. Not a one tasted as good as the real thing!

Recipe | **FRIED SQUIRREL**

Skin, dress and cut up meat in four quarters. Put in a boiling pail and parboil for about fifteen minutes. Remove and wipe dry on a cloth. Place in smoking hot skillet with plenty of hot fat. Some people prefer to have meats of this type rolled in corn meal or cracker crumbs. Take the yolks of two or three eggs and add four or five tablespoons of cracker crumbs. Mix together and dip pieces of meat in batter before placing in the hot fat. Fry until brown.

Recipe | **NORTH WOODS LIMA BEANS**

Wash dried lima beans, cover with water and hang over slow bed of coals to simmer until beans are just about done. Then add one can of tomatoes, a little chopped onion, salt and pepper, and sprinkle grated cheese over the top. Set in front of a slow back log to bake. 🍴

CHAPTER 31

Camp Kitty, a True Tale with Recipes from North Lake

SOME ENAMEL, iron, tin, and aluminum cookware and crockery form a decorative display of old-timey cooking outfits in my camp. There are a bread pan, a coffee pot, plates, bowls, cups, fry pans, pans with handles, cooking pots, and what I think are hand-painted clay pieces. They are impractical to use. Metal items have seams and soldered joints that probably leaked. Some were probably stamped out of a single piece of steel.

I learned the aluminum pieces were made from a special hard alloy. When trying to age the samples, I referred to an Abercrombie & Fitch 1903 catalog that sold camp outfits. It described aluminum cookware as retaining "all the essential properties of the pure metal, to which are added greater hardness and stiffness, making it much more durable."

I picked up the majority of the kitchen utensil parade during bushwhacks. There was a period of time during my research of the vast Moose River Plains and North Lake territories when I was determined to find the location of every known former Adirondack lumber and sportsmen's camp. A majority of those investigations began from my base camp when I rented Nat Foster Lodge.

A wire egg basket holds some early kitchen utensils. *Public Domain*

One afternoon during an all-day rainstorm I spent a good portion of my time thumbing through the former owner's camp log books and baking on the green porcelain propane kitchen range. It had a retro look. I figured it dated back to the 1920s or '30s. My daybook reminds me I experimented with what ingredients I found on the shelf and in the refrigerator. I prepared a simple potage and a dessert. What I named Brooks Lumber Camp Soup progressed from the meat on hand.

Recipe | **BROOKS LUMBER CAMP SOUP**

Ingredients:

1½ pounds of hamburger.

2 onions-diced.

2 28-ounce cans of stewed tomatoes.

[One was Italian Style. It included basil, garlic and oregano.]

3 stalks celery, chopped.

1 large can beef broth.

2 tablespoons steak sauce.

2 tablespoons curry powder.

Salt and pepper.

[*Optional ingredients could be other vegetables and a can of mushrooms with the juice.*]

Directions: Brown the hamburger and break into small pieces. Add all the ingredients in a large covered pot and cook until tender.

The dessert was a family recipe I'd read about but never tried. Since it was summer and I had an abundance of zucchini, I found my Garden Zucchini Bars were a good use of an abundant crop.

Recipe | **GARDEN ZUCCHINI BARS**

Ingredients:

zucchini, enough to make 8 cups [peeled, seeded and chopped].

⅔ cup lemon juice.

1 cup sugar.

1 teaspoon cinnamon.

1 teaspoon nutmeg.

Nat Foster's kitchen is seen through the door left of the fireplace.
Photo by Wayne and Linda Cripe. Author's Collection

4 cups flour.

1½ cups (3 sticks) butter, softened.

1½ cups sugar.

Directions: Combine zucchini, lemon juice, sugar, cinnamon, and nutmeg in a sauce pan and cook until sugar is dissolved. In a separate bowl, combine flour, butter, and sugar. Mix together evenly. Take half of the dough mixture and spread on a cookie sheet or jelly roll pan with sides. Pat down to make a crust. Bake at 350°F. for 10 minutes. Spread cooled zucchini mixture over crust. Take remaining dough and crumble on top. Bake at 350°F. for 40 minutes or until golden brown.

★ ★ ★

IT WAS AN ODD combination of events that led me put together the true Nat Foster Lodge tale about a camp kitty.

A few days earlier I had picked through the ruins of the Brooks Lumber Camp on an investigative hike to Goose Neck Lake. Then, during the rain storm, as I read this notation Rev. Byron-Curtiss made in his Nat Foster Lodge Log Book on Saturday, May 19, 1935, a chain reaction began.

> *Joseph, [his son] and Gladys Buttling were united in marriage at 4 o'clock in St. Francis Xavier Church in Brooklyn, N.Y. The couple will reside in Mt. Vernon, N.Y. Joseph promised within a month they would 'honeymoon' at North Lake.*

The entry led me to some of The Reverend's papers. Those papers led me to some snapshots of his daughter-in-law and son, while my cooking on the camp's old kitchen range using cookware he had left in camp made me think about a decades-old camp event that seemed to tickle The Reverend's funny bone.

THE GROOM KEPT his promise, and about a month later, he and Gladys returned to North Lake. When Rev. Byron-Curtiss and Joseph set out on a trek to Horn Lake, they left the new bride sleeping peacefully. Gladys awoke in the remote cabin, far from the metropolitan noise, bustle and the madcap pace she was accustomed to. Instead of the surroundings of lower Manhattan, she heard only a deep silence broken occasionally by the courting calls of newly-arrived birds, the rustling of leaves in the breeze, and water lapping against the shoreline.

Although she was alone, Gladys was looking forward to the day that lay before her. Joseph had taught her how to use the wood stove and had cautioned her not to leave food outside, since the wildlife, especially skunk and bear, could be counted on to come looking for an easy meal. Camps were often easy pickings.

Gladys's day began easily enough. She sat on the porch and sipped her morning tea, took a leisurely walk around the yard noting all of her father-in-law's construction accomplishments, investigated St. Catherine's Outdoor Chapel, and ended at the dock. The lakeside view was serene, the silence broken only by the infrequent purr from an outboard motor and a small group of quacking ducks looking for a handout. Her interest in sunbathing later in the day evaporated when nasty deerflies began to buzz around.

Joseph had described the camp as peaceful but Spartan. North Lake with all its early summer gifts was a world apart from Wall Street, where she and her husband worked. "Hours of unsurpassable happiness," she jotted on a postcard with a photo captioned "Nat Foster Lodge, Adirondacks" that she planned to mail.

Gladys put her own imprint on the camp by tidying the interior and adding the feminine touches of fresh wildflowers to the harvest table and an artful rearrangement of the bric-a-brac on the fireplace mantle.

Anticipating Gladys's arrival, and wanting to share all he loved, her father-in-law had put together a primer on woods lore. She read the names of the surrounding trees and learned to identify some. She knew the most common birds and animals. Of most interest were the many camp diaries she thumbed through at great length.

Later in the day a youthful skunk pawed at the dirt in the worm pit beyond the outhouse. She didn't hear its approach through the underbrush. The tiny young creature stepped silently. She first noticed it when she exited the outhouse, but she didn't know it was a skunk. Gladys had been alerted to stay clear of wild animals, but what serious trouble could result from one little body? Droplets of drink and morsels of food were offered on her fingertip. The little animal begged for more. Gladys might have assumed that tameness would automatically follow proffered food.

The innocent good-will gesture was fodder for another North Lake tale. In retelling it many times, Joseph said, "A skunk had surely thrown the monkey wrench into the newlywed business."

It Was Not a Pretty Kitty!

After a heavy downpour caused the men to return from their expedition, they inquired how Gladys had spent her first day at camp. Gladys enthusiastically told them all that she had done. When she spoke of meeting a little black and white "cat" that had just come from the worm pit where the garbage was turned into the soil, her listeners exchanged worried looks.

If you ever catch yourself dreaming about the good old days, just remind yourself of how kitchens used to be without all of its labor-saving cooking equipment.
Courtesy Town of Webb Historical Association

"I called, 'Here kitty cat; here pretty kitty.' It started toward me but then stopped so I went into the cabin and got some leftovers from the icebox and made some sugar water," she related.

At this point Joseph and Byron-Curtiss were fascinated, waiting to hear how it had all turned out.

"I was as peaceful as I could be and sure enough the kitty came to me. As I kneeled down and held my hand out with my fingers dripping with sugar water it licked the fingers one by one until it was all gone. Then it ate the leftovers. It must have been really hungry. When the food was gone I walked back to the kitchen and the kitty followed me in. After looking around some it went under the kitchen range, and nothing I have done has coaxed it out. I think it must be frightened."

"Holy Cow and all the Saints in Heaven! You mean you let a skunk in the camp? Where is it now?" blustered Joseph.

"A skunk!! Oh my, my, my ... Well, it's still under the range."

Byron-Curtiss chimed in, "Well, I'll be...I've had chipmunks and squirrels and, of course, mice, but never have I had the privilege of having a skunk in camp."

Joseph Byron-Curtiss's contribution to supper.
Courtesy Thomas and Doris Kilbourn (The A. L. Byron-Curtiss Collection)

So the brave men set about rousting the beast out of the dwelling. As the men carefully nudged the animal, it struggled to hide deeper in the ever-diminishing space beneath the kitchen range. At long last the agitated skunk stood bold and alert behind the rear cast iron leg, using it as the only convenient and advantageous barrier from which it could spy on its disturbers before it pounced out from under its hiding place, bolted out the open door and disappeared beneath the camp.

Joseph advised, "You can be too kind to wildlife, especially the young ones."

When Bette and I vacationed at Nat Foster Lodge, our appetites for both wilderness and camp food were whetted. Meals prepared in the setting of social history seem to enhance the experience. We did not, however, entertain any romantic ideas about the lakeside environment and The Reverend's ancient camp. Hot, humid spells brought out vicious blackflies and deerflies. Trying to sleep in the old building only resulted in waiting anxiously for daylight—my wife would characterize it as remaining on sentry duty—to arrest the chewing, scampering and scratching activities of a gross infestation of mice. As I look back, we might have traded one small skunk under the stove for all the maddening mice.

As a tribute to Joseph, Gladys, and The Reverend, I've chosen to end their camp tale with three recipes that reflect their tastes and are named after favorite Adirondack destinations they frequented.

Recipe | **MIDDLE BRANCH FALLS PICNIC DELIGHT**

Gladys Buttling Byron-Curtiss enjoyed picnics near the
second falls near the head of the Middle Branch inlet.
Ingredients:

3 apples cored [unpeeled] and cut into 1-inch pieces
(about four cups). [Granny Smith are recommended.]
2 cups whole fresh cranberries.
¾ cup sugar.
1½ cups old-fashioned oats [not quick-cook].
½ cup packed light-brown sugar.
⅛ cup all-purpose flour.
½ cup chopped pecans.
½ cup unsalted butter, melted.

Directions: Preheat oven to 350°F. Butter a 2-quart baking dish. Next, in a large bowl , mix together the apples, cranberries, and sugar. Spoon into prepared baking dish. In the same bowl, mix together the oats, brown sugar, flour, and pecans. Stir in the melted butter. Finally, sprinkle the oatmeal mixture evenly over the top of the apples. Bake at 350°F. for 45 minutes until bubbly and apples are tender. Serve warm or cold with a scoop of ice cream, or whipped cream, if desired.

A logging bridge spans Middle Branch Falls stream. *Author's Collection*

BLACK RIVER TROUT IN TOMATO SAUCE

Rev. Byron-Curtiss had a fondness for trout.

Ingredients:

2 pounds fish fillet (trout or salmon).

½ cup chopped onion.

2 cups tomato sauce.

1 bay leaf.

1 teaspoon sugar.

flour.

salt and pepper to taste.

¼ cup white wine.

Directions: Sprinkle salt and pepper on fish fillets, dip in flour and cook in oil on both sides until done. Remove fish from skillet and keep warm. In same skillet cook onion in a little oil until tender but not brown. Add tomato sauce and wine, bay leaf, sugar, salt and pepper to taste; cook 5 minutes more. For serving, arrange fish filets and sauce alternately. Can be served cold or warm. Serves 4.

Recipe **JOSEPH'S WOLF MOUNTAIN MEAT DELIGHT**

Joseph Byron-Curtiss enjoyed tasty main dishes that used leftovers.

Ingredients:

½ pound ground beef.

½ pound ground veal.

¼ pound ground pork.

1 beaten egg.

¼ cup water.

1 teaspoon salt.

Dash of pepper.

8 slices bacon.

Directions: Mix meats; add egg, water, and seasonings. Mix well and pat ½-inch thick on waxed paper. Spread with Bread Stuffing; roll as for jelly roll. Place in greased baking pan; cover with bacon slices. Bake in moderate oven (350°F.) 1 hour. Garnish with buttered whole onions, parsnips, and parsley. Serves 6 to 8.

Low mountains surround North Lake. *Photo by Wayne and Linda Cripe. Author's Collection*

Recipe BREAD STUFFING

Ingredients:

3 cups dry bread cubes.

2 tablespoons chopped onion.

¼ cup seedless raisins.

¼ cup chopped celery.

Salt and pepper.

½ teaspoon sage.

½ cup canned bouillon or 1 bouillon cube in ½ cup water.

Directions: Combine ingredients and mix well.

CHAPTER 32

Sweet Squash and Acorn Charley

Recipe — **CHARLEY'S SWEET STUFFED SQUASH**

Ingredients:

2 large (1¼-to-1½- pound size) acorn squashes.

2 tablespoons butter or margarine.

⅛ cup maple syrup.

¼ cup dark seedless raisins.

¾ pound boiled ham in one piece, cut into ½-inch cubes.

2 packages (5⅞-ounce size) frozen apple-pecan rice.
[An alternative not kitchen-tested might be to cook 1 cup of rice using one cup apple juice and one cup water, and add ½ cup of chopped pecans. It would make 3 cups cooked rice. Each squash half would probably hold ¾ cup.]

1 red apple, cored and sliced.

Directions: Cut each acorn squash in half lengthwise; remove and discard seeds and fibers. In a 13-by-9 –inch microwave-safe baking dish, place squash halves, cut sides down. Cover with plastic wrap, turning back a corner to vent. Microwave at HIGH (100% power) 10 minutes. Turn halves cut sides up. (Squash should be for-tender. If not, microwave longer.) Place 1½ tea-spoons butter in each cavity; recover with plastic wrap.

In medium-size glass bowl, combine maple syrup and raisins. Cover with plastic wrap; vent. Microwave at HIGH 3 minutes, stirring once. Toss ham cubes with raisin mixture; set aside.

and The Adirondack Characters Who Cooked Them Up

With fork, pierce the frozen rice pouches. Cook pierced side up on HIGH 3 minutes, rearranging after 1½ minutes. Cut pouches open; toss rice with ham mixture; fill squash cavities, dividing evenly. Cover loosely with plastic wrap; microwave at HIGH 1½ minutes. Transfer to serving dishes; garnish with apple slices and, if desired, parsley.

Makes 4 servings.

Note: this recipe was cooked in a 600–700-watt microwave oven. If you prefer not to cover food with plastic wrap [I normally use wax paper] an alternative is to cook halved squash for about 45 minutes at 400 degrees. I put an inch of water in the bottom of a pan and cover with foil so they're steaming as well as baking. Then after the shells are filled they could go back in the oven for 10 minutes or so.

SWEET ACORN CHARLEY

Nicknames were often recorded in the Nat Foster log books. For more on these personalities, please read my *Adirondack Stories of the Black River Country or Under an Adirondack Influence: The Life of A. L. Byron-Curtiss, 1871–1959.* Many men and women spent time with Rev. Byron-Curtiss at North Lake. B-C, as The Reverend referred to himself in camp log books, often gave his friends labels with noteworthy monikers. Dubbing came about from a particular claim; a trapping, hunting or fishing experience; a memorable event; any number of other amusing or odd peculiarities. Rev. Byron-Curtiss himself had many names: the Commodore, His Eminence, the Dominie, the Keeper of the Log, The Loggist, the Bishop of North Lake, the Pope and the Ex-Pope of North Lake's chapel.

"Sweet Acorn" Charley was an oft-mentioned moniker in the first Nat Foster Lodge log book. A picture of the old feller standing in the State House clearing stuffing his mouth with shredded Sweet Acorn tobacco manufactured by C.J. Aldridge of Rome, N.Y., confirms why he was dubbed "Sweet Acorn." It's also easy to picture him arriving at camp: his work completed for the week, he rowed across the water, beached the boat, and perhaps walked more swiftly than he had all day to The Reverend's cabin door. B-C might greet him with, "Well, Sweet Acorn, what you got in that bottle tucked under your arm?"

"SWEET ACORN'S" WILD CAPER STEAK SPECIALTY

Charley's easy-to-make, homey, exotic, camp-sounding dish with a tasty stuffing is nothing more than a glorified Hungarian Schrazy. Yet, his recipe title smacks of an Adirondack wholesomeness. It was a meal Rev. Byron-Curtiss and he enjoyed. —The Author

Ingredients:

1 pound round steak, cut in 4 serving-size pieces
(Charley used deer meat.)

1 medium-sized onion, chopped

1 green pepper, chopped (½ cup)

¾ cup grated raw carrot

3 slices of bacon, chopped
(Charley used ⅛ pound of salt pork.)

Salt and pepper to taste

1 cup boiling water

Directions: Pound flour into meat with a meat mallet or the side of a sturdy plate; season with salt and pepper. Combine remaining ingredients except water. Place small amount on each piece of meat. Roll; tie securely with string. (Charley used old fishing line! Use string. Monofilament line will melt.) Brown in hot fat or salad oil. Add water; cover and simmer 1½ hours. Thicken stock for gravy. Remove string from the meat rolls. (Charley failed to include that direction.) Pour gravy over the meat. Serves 4.

"Sweet Acorn" Charley.
Courtesy Thomas and Doris Kilbourn (The A. L. Byron-Curtiss Collection)

Rev. Byron-Curtiss saved Charles's tobacco label in his 1902 camp log book.

Courtesy Thomas and Doris Kilbourn (The A. L. Byron-Curtiss Collection)

Spring Trout & Strawberry Pancakes: Borrowed Tales, Quirky Cures, Camp Recipes

May was black fly season, and with the winged critters thicker than molasses, the two men would cozy up in their long-sleeved work shirts and caps and lean idly on the wooden arms of rocking chairs to enjoy a leisurely exchange of the hamlet of Atwell's happenings of the day. An empty Gibson's Linseed Liquorice and Menthol Cough Lozenges tin set by the rear of the cold cast-iron wood stove received frequent squirts of tobacco juice, along with an occasional quid which had served its time. Pipe tobacco from a glass canister in the middle of a pipe rack gave B-C, a non-tobacco chewer, something to smoke. The men would take turns telling stories.

At 3 o'clock Sunday afternoon Acorn might announce, "Well, I guess I best be getting home. You know how cranky ole 'Silver Top' gets when I'm not on time for supper. The occasion can make for a rough house."

The Reverend knew Acorn's wife, Ethel, from his St. Joseph's parish in Rome. Acorn took liberties when vacationing at camp that he would never get away with in his home. Rev. Byron-Curtiss has mentioned in his papers that Ethel had "rare talents and an authoritative way about her." Sweet Acorn, on the other hand, has been described as having a "twinkle of blended mischief and kind-heartedness" on his weathered face. Acorn and The Reverend enjoyed each other's company on trips to the Adirondacks. B-C said, "During those rides he filled my head with stories of the old days."

Based on speculation, I pictured B-C and Acorn standing, stretching wearily, and walking down to the dock. Acorn knew that in order for peace and harmony to reign in his house, he'd best be moving along. Ethel's reputation with a double-barrel shotgun was well-known. Once, when at camp with her husband, she commanded him to come to supper with a double shell blast over the water.

The friends would bid "good-day" and return to their individual lives, happily anticipating their next meeting at the lake to fish Grindstone Creek or another favorite fishing hole.

Oh, and just for the record, Sweet Acorn Charley real name was Michael Apple—really!

In addition to Ethel's reputation for feistiness, she was known for her meat dishes that ranged from simple to gourmet. Ethel's fish-vegetable pie was one of Rev. Byron-Curtiss' favorite meals.

Recipe NORTH WOODS FISH-VEGETABLE PIE

This was a camp guest favorite at Nat Foster Lodge.

Ingredients:

1 pound fish fillets, cut in 1-inch pieces.

6 carrots, diced.

4 medium potatoes, diced.

4 medium onions, sliced.

1 teaspoon salt.

3 tablespoons butter or margarine.

3 tablespoons flour.

1½ cups milk.

¼ teaspoon pepper.

Baking-powder-biscuit dough.

Directions: Cook fish and vegetables in boiling salted water 10 minutes, or until vegetables are just tender. Drain; reserve liquid, adding water if necessary to make 1½ cups. Melt butter and blend in flour. Add liquid from vegetables, the milk, salt and pepper, and cook, stirring until thickened. Put fish and vegetables in greased 9-inch round or square baking dish and pour on sauce and top with rounds of biscuit dough. Bake at 400°F. about 20 minutes. Makes 4 servings.

Recipe MOUNTAIN CLAM CHOWDER

A surprisingly easy and inexpensive modern recipe with a taste of the sea. Old time guides who were invited by wealthy patrons to New York City and a meal on the town might have enjoyed a similar soup at Delmonico's. This home-cooked reminder of their big-city spree was a fine prelude to the kettle of venison ribs and onions that might follow.

Ingredients:

2 tablespoons olive oil.

2–3 slices bacon, diced.

1 large onion, chopped.

Salt and pepper.

2 cloves garlic, finely chopped.

2 tablespoon flour.

Two 6.5-ounce cans chopped clams in clam juice.

One 8-ounce bottle clam juice.

3 cups whole milk.

1 pound medium red potatoes, cut into ½ inch pieces.

6 sprigs fresh thyme.

One 10-ounce package frozen corn, thawed,

or one 16-oz. can corn.

Additional cooked crumbled bacon and

chopped parsley, for serving.

Directions: Place the oil and bacon in a large pot and cook over medium heat, stirring occasionally, until the bacon is crisp, about 5 minutes.

Add the onion, season with ¼ teaspoon salt and ½ teaspoon pepper and cook, covered, stirring occasionally, until very tender, 8 to 10 minutes. Stir in the garlic and cook for 1 minute.

Sprinkle the flour over the onion and cook, stirring, for 1 minute. Drain the canned clam juice into the pan (reserve the clams), add the bottled clam juice and stir to combine.

Stir in the milk, then add the potatoes and thyme and bring the mixture to a boil, stirring occasionally. Reduce heat and simmer for 12 minutes. Add the corn and clams and cook until the potatoes are just tender and the corn and clams are heated through, about 3 minutes.

Discard the thyme and serve the soup with crumbled bacon and parsley, if desired, or serve topped with herb or garlic croutons. ☕

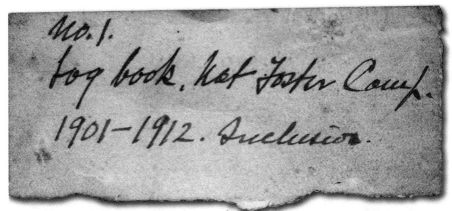

Camp log books provide a historic record.

CHAPTER 33

A Very BIG Frog and
Favorite Celia's Favorite Food

A CENTURY AGO, many campers enjoyed gathering wild foods, and they fished and hunted. Camp life gave them an opportunity to live somewhat off the land. Some of the wild foods once popular are not common to 21st—century folks. However, a hundred years ago spring greens like dandelion, cowslips, lamb's quarter, pokeberry, nettles, horseradish leaves, milkweed sprouts, and "scurvy grass" or smooth mustard were part of an average person's camp diet.

Gathering didn't stop with green leaves, stems, and roots. They would pick wild strawberries, fill milk and lard pails with black and red raspberries, and harvest small wild blueberries that grew along streams and along the fringes of bogs and wet areas that were exposed to full sunlight. Too frequently the gatherers competed with black bears, who also enjoyed the succulence of the sugary pea-size blueberries. Ladies in camp baked delicious berry shortcakes dripping with crushed berries and sweet cream.

Otto Horan Jr. remembers one memorable camp vacation when he accompanied his mother on a berry expedition: "While bathing in the lake with my friends Victor and Joe, I stepped on a broken booze bottle. It left a rather large gash on the bottom of my foot. It was my good fortune a medical doctor was vacationing at a neighboring camp. He tailored the injury up with cat gut.

"My mother was upset about the injury, but the event had a happy ending. Not only did the doctor treat me, but I was distracted from the surgery

The thrill of picking the berry grounds was to see how quickly pails filled up. One stand-by snack was bread and butter overspread with a layer of berries and sugar and patted down with little fingers. *Courtesy of George Shaughnessy*

that needed to be performed by the stories told to me by several of the people in camp."

These are the stories Otto remembered hearing. Celia Stapleton's tale follows.

"Otto, you should have seen the exceptional bull frog I caught sight of as I walked past the stagnant water near Devil's Brook. I'm positive it was more or less as big as the bullfrog Henry Paull caught earlier in the summer. He was so proud of the trophy find that he sent it down to a taxidermist in Utica to be mounted. It was shipped live by express freight. Why, that mount cost him two dollars and seventy-five cents! I'm told that amphibian critter must have weighed at least thirty pounds!"

Otto's father enjoyed the serenity of the Adirondack woodlands.
Courtesy Town of Webb Historical Association

Spring Trout & Strawberry Pancakes: Borrowed Tales, Quirky Cures, Camp Recipes

An Adirondack League Club party. Guide Giles Becraft is second from left.
Courtesy Helen Becraft Wheatley

Not to be outdone, and to keep Otto's mind off the sutures the doctor threaded to pull the deep wound together, Otto Jr. said his father spun this yarn.

"One time when I was staying overnight in the old cook shanty, at Perry's old Number 1 lumber camp, one of the men in my deer hunting party came into the kitchen carrying a heavy piece of meat for supper. I compared it to the size of a leg of lamb. Well, we all dug into that mass of meat and kept eating until we thought we'd pop our suspender buttons. It tasted as good as any mutton I ever had, too.

"By and by I asked Lon, who was our camp cook, what sort of meat it was. In all likelihood you won't believe me, but Lon told us it was one of those South Lake frogs that had come downstream and gotten into Bull Moose Swamp. And he'd only cooked up one of its hind legs of course!"

Otto told me, "Celia Stapleton was not a woman to be outdone in the tall tale." She had heard the men swap stories at camp for years.

Not only was Celia known to be a good storyteller but she had a reputation at the lake as expert cook. "My folks spoke of her as 'a culinary artist,'" said Otto. "My father used to talk about the surprise meal Mrs. S. cooked for him to celebrate his thirty-ninth birthday. The pie was from red raspberries and blackberries we kids gathered and then there was dad's favorite pork and beans, cabbage and wild greens."

Following Otto's tangent, he relit his pipe and gazed thoughtfully into space before continuing.

"She told my father, 'That's some big frog, all right, Otto, but it couldn't have been more than the little grandson of the frog I saw in Little Woodhull Lake. Now, that was some frog! Mr. Watkins was guiding me and his wife, Agnes, that day. We were both fishing from a log raft while Ira poled. All of a sudden I heard Ira begin to utter up at breakneck speed.

"'What's that over there?'" he cried as he pointed toward the point where a little shack was setting.

"Agnes's and my eyes darted in the direction he pointed. What we saw were a pair of eyeballs setting up even with the surface of the water, and those round eyes were the size of the face of my Baby Ben alarm clock—each one of them! Well, we kept watching, as Ira moved the raft closer. Fairly soon we understood that it was one of those Goliath Little Woodhull frogs, sitting on the mud bottom of the lake with its head just above the water. Now I want to tell you, that was a full-grown frog, because Ira got out his line and sinker and measured the depth of the water. You know it was exactly thirty-seven feet deep!"

These yarns are some of the tales I have enjoyed collecting during the search for old-time recipes and tall stories. Otto ended by telling me the ones he remembered were "all true...to some degree."

Otto's tales were tall and as broad as the maple trees he tapped. The following recipes are modern versions of Celia's old fashioned favorites.

Recipe	CELIA'S MAPLE NUT PIE

Ingredients:

1¼ cups packed brown sugar.

½ cup whipping cream.

⅛ cup maple syrup.

1 egg.

2 tablespoons butter.

½ cup chopped nut—walnuts, pecans or whatever is on hand.

9-inch shell, partially baked.

Directions: In a large bowl, beat together the brown sugar, cream, maple syrup, egg, and butter until smooth. Fold in the nuts. Pour into the lightly browned pie shell. Bake in a 350°F. oven for 45 minutes or until the crust is golden and the filing is set. Cool on a wire rack. Serves 6 to 8. Top with cinnamon-spiced whipped cream.

Recipe **CINNAMON-SPICED WHIPPED CREAM**

Pour one cup of heavy whipping cream into a cold bowl and whip until soft peaks form. Keep whipping while you add two table-spoons of sugar and one teaspoon cinnamon. Serve immediately.

Recipe **RASPBERRY SALAD**

Ingredients:
1 large package of raspberry Jello®.
2 cups boiling water.
2 (10 ounce) packages of frozen raspberries in juice, thawed.
1 (16 ounce) jar natural, unsweetened applesauce.
Directions: Dissolve gelatin in boiling water thoroughly; cool until just beginning to set. Add thawed berries and juice along with applesauce. Pour into large mold or bowl and chill until firm. Serve with dressing, if desired (see below).

Recipe **DRESSING FOR RASPBERRY SALAD**

Ingredients:
½ pint sour cream.
16 large or 1½ cups miniature marshmallows.
Directions: Soak marshmallows overnight in sour cream. Beat until smooth.
(*This dressing could be used for any Jello® salad.*)

Recipe **PERRY'S CAMP BAKED CABBAGE CASSEROLE**

Ingredients:
1 medium cabbage, shredded.
1 onion, chopped.

1 pound of lean hamburger.

1 cup uncooked rice (not instant).

Salt and pepper.

1½ cups boiling water.

½ stick margarine.

1 8-ounce can tomato sauce.

Directions: Spread one-half cabbage into a greased casserole. Fry onion in margarine. Add rice and brown. Pour over cabbage. Brown hamburger and spread over rice. Add salt and pepper. Mix water with the tomato sauce. Pour over the top of the remaining cabbage. Cover. Bake at 350°F. ⚓

Forest Lodge on the shore of Jock's Lake, renamed Honnedaga Lake by the A.L.C. The Adirondack League Club's formation in 1890 began with a "purchase of more than ninety thousand acres of area land, the western line cutting North Lake in two and running as far north as a mile or two short of the Fulton Chain of Lakes." —Thomas C. O'Donnell. *Courtesy Helen Becraft Wheatley*

CHAPTER 34

Hair-Growing Trout

THIS STORY comes from Father McNeill, the former Catholic priest in charge of St. Joseph's Church in Boonville and St. Patrick's Church in Forestport. He had a knack for storytelling along with spreading the word to the faithful.

I don't know if anyone has ever heard of the barber pole method of fishing in recent times. I certainly wouldn't challenge the pastor's claim.

In the days before yesterday it happened that there was a backwoods hamlet in the Adirondacks where a majority of the woodsmen were bald. A dynamic hair tonic peddler from Utica resolved to take an interest and profit from this favorable opening by taking a wagon trip to the deep-woods community of Wheelertown.

The weather turned awful during the peddler's northward journey. What began as a light rain soon turned to one of those intense North Country thunder-boomers. As the snake oil peddler was crossing the bridge over the Black River at Bellingertown, heading toward Pony Bob's, an unusual rattling noise caused by the wagon wheels turning on the wooden planks of the bridge just as a boom of thunder sounded caused the horse to spook. The animal broke from its usual trot into high speed. With a quick jerk on the reins, the salesman let out a loud yell, rose clear off his seat and did all he could to control the terrified horse.

The driver was quick, but he could not completely steady the spooked animal. The horse, quivering with fear, slipped on the wet boards, causing the wagon to slide sideways and hit the side of the bridge. Four cases of hair tonic toppled over in the wagon box. The glass jars broke and the liquid cascaded all over. The rig's left rear wheel smashed against the abutment and tore off, resulting in the rig tipping over. The liquid content spilled into the river.

It wasn't long after the accident that fishermen along the Black River developed a novel fishing technique. They would stake out their favorite fishing spot by driving in a miniature red and white striped pole with painted barber shears, comb, and razor. Once anglers had placed their pole in the shallows of the river's edge, they would call out: "*Get your free haircut and trim your beard here!*" All the trout whose hair had grown too long or who needed a shave or trim would beat a path right up to the pole where they could be picked up.

Fish and deer meat were everyday table fare at Adirondack tables.
Courtesy Town of Webb Historical Association

  Spring Trout & Strawberry Pancakes: Borrowed Tales, Quirky Cures, Camp Recipes

The menu at the Higby Club at Big Moose Lake included trout. "A conscientious [hotel] operator wants to serve the best possible meals and provide good service to his customers. To do this is to invite repeat business, and fill one's house with desirable guests."—Roy Higby. *Courtesy Town of Webb Historical Association*

The practice of fishing that way came to an end after the flood of April 21, 1869, when the dam at North Lake gave way and sent a wall of water rushing down the valley. It muddied the waters and filled the shoreline with debris, making it impossible for the fish to see the barber poles.

★ ★ ★

THE SIMPLEST, and some say the tastiest, way to cook those freshly-caught trout right on the shore is to simply gut and wash them, wrap a few slices of bacon around each fish, and then wrap individually in foil. Bake in hot coals for twenty minutes or so.

For those who didn't care for fish, Richard Smith often prepared this popular recipe with the ever-present Daisy Ham.

BEAR TRAP CAMP HAM LOAF

Ingredients:

2½ lbs. ground ham.

1 can cracker crumbs.

1 egg.

1 cup milk.

Pepper to taste.

1 teaspoon baking powder.

Directions: Mold in bread tin and pour the following over the top: 1 cup sugar, 2 teaspoons prepared mustard and ½ cup cider vinegar. Bake at 300°F. for 1½ hours. Serve with sauce made of whipped cream, horseradish and mayonnaise. (Smith's recipe book doesn't tell how much.)

Smith said the following recipe was a breakfast favorite of his when he spent time at his Bear Trap camp in the Adirondacks. He offered no specific instructions, but said simply that it is easy to bake. The assumption is the sweet confectionary relied on the skill of the baker.

ADIRONDACK COFFEE CAKE

½ cup sugar.

¼ cup butter.

1 egg.

¼ cup milk.

1 cup flour.

1 teaspoon baking powder.

Directions: Dust top of cake with cinnamon and sugar.

Here are my Best Wishes for the Year 1939. with Trout ~~Fishing~~ and Deer Hunting for recreation . –NJR

Fishing Pals

UNCLE EARL and Aunt Emma enjoyed fishing. Uncle Earl also raised worms to sell. When I visited them I looked forward to eating Aunt Emma's cookies and pulling out "the berthing" trays to look at the wiggling critters. When I work egg shells and coffee grounds into my compost pile and see the young red worms, I think of all the flats my uncle once tended. It was always easier to get worms from him than to go outside with a flashlight to pluck night crawlers. I never found one long enough to dangle over my shoulder. They must develop differently at Cold River!

Mary Dittmar and Noah John Rondeau fishing Boiling Pond (aka Seward Pond) on the hermit's homemade raft. Circa 1940s. *Courtesy of Dr. Adolph G. Dittmar, Jr.*

Fishing poles were put away when this picture was snapped by Frank Rix. These ladies found the calm water of Piseco Lake too irresistible to do anything other than to enjoy the exceptional day to paddle their canoe. *Courtesy Piseco Historical Society*

Recipe   **AUNT EMMA'S WOODSMAN'S HERMITS**

Ingredients:

⅔ cup molasses.

½ cup sugar.

½ teaspoon salt.

3 cups flour.

1 teaspoon ginger.

1 teaspoon cinnamon.

½ cup melted lard or butter.

⅔ cup boiling water.

1 cup scalded raisins or currants.

1 heaping teaspoon baking soda.

Directions: Put the molasses into a pan and boil slowly for five minutes. Add the sugar, lard, boiling water, salt and raisins. Mix well. Sift flour, baking soda, and spices together, then add to the molasses, etc., and beat thoroughly. Add enough more flour to make a moderately thin batter. Drop from spoon into well-greased tins and bake in a hot oven. 🍴

CHAPTER 36

This Trout Was Wired

AS A TEENAGER living in Herkimer, NY, Roy Wires fished mostly the lower end of West Canada Creek, limited by how far he could ride his bicycle. Middleville, about 8 miles up Route 28, was pretty much his limit. This stretch of the creek flowed mainly through farmland, and unfortunately,

Roy inherited his love of fishing from his father Edwin and grandmother Emily.
Courtesy Roy E. Wires (The Emily Mitchell Wires Collection)

Emily Mitchell Wires preparing her Tomato Wiggle.
Courtesy Roy E. Wires (The Emily Mitchell Wires Collection)

many times the creek banks became a farmer's personal junkyard. It was not unusual to see old car bodies, worn-out farm implements, barbwire, and other junk discarded over the bank. The only problem was, in times of spring thaw and the resultant high water, many of those items got washed into the creek.

It was one of those items that one day almost cost Roy a big trout. Back in the days of this story, the dam on the West Canada Creek at Trenton released water almost every afternoon to generate electric power. This of course resulted in the creek downstream of the dam rising 12 to 18 inches every afternoon and evening.

It was one of those late afternoons that Roy was spin-fishing a stretch of the creek with his favorite lure, a gold phoebe. After what had been a less than fruitful day up to this point, he hooked a nice brown trout that did a couple of cartwheels and then started digging deep. It was obvious that this brown trout knew his way around the creek; all of a sudden the line became tight. Although the fish was still hooked, as he could feel him and see an occasional flash out in the stream, Roy just couldn't get him in. The only alternative was to wade out to where he was, and see what he was hooked on.

The fish had swum through a big roll of discarded barbwire. Roy knew there was no way he could thread him out of that mess, and wondering how long his four-pound test line was going to hold up, he started letting out line, hoping it would pull him downstream and he could net him below the coil of barbwire and then once he had him in the net, he would cut his line, and pull it through. Well, this sounded like a good plan, until the water started rising from the afternoon discharge at Trenton. Roy had already just about reached the limit on his hip boots getting to the fish, and knew that the rising water would flood his boots and he was going to be in real trouble.

"Standing on my tiptoes with the water coming up rapidly," he remembered, "I was finally able to net my fish, a nice 15-inch West Canada Creek brown trout. At that point I just cut my line and headed for the bank with the trout. 'Farmer Brown's' barbwire had almost cheated me out of a real prize trout, and the Trenton discharge of water was close to closing the deal on netting that trophy. I guess the fishing gods were with me that day."

`Recipe` **ROY'S RECIPE FOR TROUT**

Heads off. Guts out. A little salt and pepper inside the body cavity; a little minced onion sprinkled inside the cavity. Set trout on a sheet of aluminum foil, put a couple of tablespoons of butter on top of trout. Bring the edges of the aluminum foil together creating a little tent, closed on the ends. Ten minutes on low heat grill or fire (depending on size). When done (test for flakiness), the butter should have melted over the trout and will help keep the cooked trout from sticking to the aluminum foil. I like a big baked potato and corn on the cob with my trout. If I'm "roughing it" and have a cast iron skillet available, there's nothing like flapjacks and trout.

Roy offers this as his mother's favorite way to cook trout:

`Recipe` **HELEN'S FAVORITE TROUT RECIPE**

Prepare trout by gutting and beheading. Pour canned tomatoes in a skillet. Lay fish on top. Sprinkle cut-up black olives and parmesan cheese with a little pepper. Simmer until fish flakes.

Roy's Grandmother Emily Wires liked to make this spread for crackers to eat while the trout was cooking:

`Recipe` **GRANDMA EMILY'S TOMATO WIGGLE**

Melt 1 tablespoon butter
Add 1 tablespoon flour.
Stir smooth and add ¾ cup canned tomatoes and some cheese cut fine. Cook until thickened. Season to taste with salt, pepper & a little sugar. Serve on crackers. 🐟

SECTION FIVE

Winding Down

THERE ISN'T ANY pure wilderness in the Adirondacks. The land has all been touched by man. What there is today, however, does feel reasonably wild. Adventures and reflections help to keep my mind close to the wilds. So do the thoughts of the meals enjoyed under a canopy of trees, sitting by an overhanging ledge of stone eating a sandwich, or standing on a dock to skip rocks across a placid sheet of water before turning and walking the wooden stairs back to camp for a last meal before packing the car to return home. There will be future opportunities to explore the hills and swamps; identify flowers, shrubs and trees; stand by a waterfall; pull a trout from the stream or return to the dock to sit and read recollections of bygone times and personalities from long ago. I like to think that sharing these stories and recipes with others will remind them of their own happy times in wild places and so some of the meals they enjoyed, and can now enjoy again.

The Conklin sisters, Harriet and Ruth, were trappers. Harriet smoked a clay pipe, drank some whiskey at times, and lived in a cabin way back in the woods.
Courtesy of the Maitland C. DeSormo Collection

CHAPTER 37

'Dacks' Crazy Season

WHEN LABOR DAY expires, the September changes take hold. Sugar maples, paper birch, beech, and cherry leaves turn a rainbow of colors. Tamarack needles develop a gold that gleams in bright sunlit days. After first frost and cold nights come warm days and cooler water and a last short timespan in the Adirondack Mountains for the late hatchings of winged insects.

Old-time campers used to call the end of September the "crazy season." You might wonder why. I've read that in the *Wilderness Trail Book*, a ninety-year-old tramp and trail companion paperback that lacks the front and back cover and the first six pages. The author told the name came from the behavior of the partridge in late September and in early October. "The wild grape, after it has been touched with frost, is a favorite food, as well as other wild fruits, much of which would have withered and dried: choke-cherries, blueberries, barberries and wild apples." When partridge feed on these fermented fruits they often act wild. They become nervous, very alert, seemingly "on edge." Often they will fly against buildings, crash into window glass, and bomb through window screening.

My best-loved outdoor trips are between the September equinox and the December solstice. It's an exceptional period of time to be out and about on the water or in the forest. The warm nights of summer are gone. Cooler water seems to renew game fishes' interest in life. The majority of anglers have stored away their rods and called it a season. Trout head up into the small headwater streams as far as they can get, where they know the feed is good for their young offspring. Leaf drop tells that another fall

Shaded by the camp's veranda, she considers the autumn foliage that decorates
the trees like an artist's pallette. The blue lake glitters with sparkling sunlight.
Courtesy Special Collections, Feinberg Library, SUNY College at Plattsburgh

and winter are on the way, and before freeze-up, perhaps taking their cue from the loud lonesome chirp of the crickets on the land, the trout then reverse their direction. They swim downstream back toward the nearest lake or pond — back into deep water, going down into deep holes, lying pretty close to the bottom and feeding on minnows and freshwater smelt, insect life such as the mason caducei fly, and small bits of vegetable matter.

Late fall, before the mating season when buck are extremely wild, finds the deer working their way up from the ponds and swamps to higher ground. There, winding their way along the hardwood ridges, they seek out favored dark green mushrooms that develop on fallen beech logs. With relish they dig among fallen leaves for the desired beechnut — an abundance of which means prosperity for many forest creatures. Deer will not abandon these feeding grounds, if beechnuts are plentiful, until a foot or more of snow covers the ground.

As the autumn closes in on winter, seasonal camp owners begin the tasks to winterize their buildings. It will soon be time to close up camp.

Food refuels the belly. Nature can be a medication. It brings peace and tranquility and beauty. It's been that strong lure that has drawn oldsters back to the wilds of their earlier days. And for those who can't make the trip, they tell me there is still a feeling of excitement and anticipation every time they think about how nice it would be to return if they only could.

At each old camp or site I've visited, as I sat there alone, sometimes eyes half closed in thought, it's not that difficult to put myself back in time with a familiar contact—sharing a meal and listening as evening stories were spun.

| Recipe | CAMP COZY'S RICE STUFFING FOR STEAMED FOWL |

Ingredients:
1 cup dry rice (pre-cooked).
1 cup finely chopped celery.
¼ cup minced celery leaves.
¼ cup minced onions.
2 tablespoons of parsley.
1 teaspoon salt.
⅛ teaspoon pepper.
¼ teaspoon poultry seasoning.

Directions: Stuff fowl, sew up and truss. Place breast down in kettle. Add ½ cup water and ¼ teaspoons salt per lb. Add neck and gizzard to water. Cook liver separately. Bring to boil quickly, then reduce heat. Cover and simmer until tender (about 3 hours). Turn chicken when half done. Place in pan and put into a hot oven to brown. 🍷

Jay O'Hern on an autumn investigative bushwhack. *Author's Photo*

"When the leaves are off the trees, And the honey from the bees
Sweetens up your morning cup of tea, You watch its steam arise
Like the fog into the skies, Grab your hat and coat and walk with me."
    —*Mountain Air.* Used by permission © 1987 Dan Berggren/Berggren Music, BMI

CHAPTER 38

A Picnic on Ice Cave Mountain

IT HAS BEEN a long time since I first summited Ice Cave Mountain for a look at the so-called "ice cave" on the peak and a picnic overlooking the balancing rock. I've taken many hikes to it since then. It's a favorite late spring or fall trip, but not a destination recommended during the buggy portion of the year.

A reporter, Linda Murphy, and photographer, Heather Ainsworth, from the Utica *Observer-Dispatch* accompanied me on a trip to the summit one autumn day. Their actions provided me some silent laughter. I had cautioned the women to dress appropriately and to be prepared to trek over a blind path—my term for an unmarked but visible (to a degree) pathway. They seemed in high spirits and alert to hazards until they realized a fact I had not paid any attention to. Almost in unison they exclaimed, "We're in the wilderness!" When I asked what they meant, they pointed to their cell phones. They were not getting any reception. I suggested something along the lines of trying to concentrate on the beauty of the surroundings rather than the stark terror of an afternoon without a smart phone.

I remember that hike because of the sandwich I had experimented with as I packed my lunch that morning, because the women were good sports even when the walking turned rough. Irregularities became hidden traps, branches slapped them when they walked too close to each other, and briers clawed at their clothing. As I enjoyed a leisurely rest and late lunch, they commented that they were going to see where their cell phone reception would pick on their way out of the woods.

The reporters seemed uninterested in the gourmet sandwiches I'd brought for them, not really tasting them as they held their phones up in various directions, still perplexed and dismayed by their disconnection with civilization.

As we passed the North Lake sluiceway I pointed out the boarded-up State House and told a story about Anna Brown, a locally known cook. Patrons raved about her table fare and often left with a favorite recipe to try in their own kitchens. Summer residents and campers all raved about her Sunday standard of eggs, bacon, and biscuits with chicken gravy, a breakfast she used to serve in the large dining room.

Elated teenagers pose on the summit of Ice Cave Mountain after finding the famous Ice Cave. Circa 1930s. *Courtesy Thomas and Doris Kilbourn (The A. L. Byron-Curtiss Collection)*

Opposite: On the heels of numerous newspaper reports about women exploring for the deposit of perpetual ice "caused by convulsion of nature," written by Rev. Byron-Curtiss, the stories attracted the attention of adventurous people. The Reverend offered all who would bring a sample of the ice to his camp a notarized statement of success and a picnic at his lodge. *Courtesy Thomas and Doris Kilbourn (The A. L. Byron-Curtiss Collection)*

I wondered what Anna might have thought about my cold sandwich. Knowing her wizardry, I think she would have given it a thumbs up. I know I did. I wrote it down, too—with a pen, on a recipe card.

`Recipe` **ORANGE-BEEF SANDWICH**

Ingredients:

¾ pound roast beef, sliced thin.

½ teaspoon rosemary, crumbled.

Salt to taste.

1 cup orange juice.

3 crusty sandwich rolls, split and toasted if desired.

Ginger Mayonnaise.

Lettuce leaves.

Directions: In 8-inch square glass baking dish, arrange meat slices in single layer and sprinkle with a little rosemary and salt. Repeat layers, then pour orange juice over meat, cover and refrigerate 1 to 2 hours. Drain well. Spread rolls with Ginger Mayonnaise. Arrange meat on roll bottoms and top with lettuce and roll tops.

`Recipe` **GINGER MAYONNAISE**

Combine ¼ cup mayonnaise and ½ teaspoon ground ginger. 🍶

Vintage photos like this 1890 scene of the road that passes over North Lake dam, helped the O-D reporters gain a feeling of Atwell in the old days. *Author's Collection*

CHAPTER 39

Welcoming Adirondack Campfire and Cast Iron Cookware

HERE'S AN INTERESTING notice from The American Angler, in June 1920.

Forest fires in the Adirondacks, which, according to dispatches from the mountain regions, have been threatening serious damage, were all reported to be either extinguished or under control…by Conservation Commissioner George D. Pratt.

Commissioner Pratt stated that those fires of which the origin was known were set as a result of carelessness on the part of fishermen, and with the prospects of continued dry weather he urges upon all anglers or other users of the woods to exercise particular caution to make sure that lighted matches or burning tobacco are not thrown upon the ground and that camp fires are carefully extinguished before they are left.[9]

Anglers during the early years of the 20th century often relied on the "Register of Guides," a publication issued by the Conservation Commission. It was one of a number of illustrated booklets that contained maps of the Adirondack, Catskill and St. Lawrence regions in color. They described all the state reservations and told of the regulations governing the use of state land including rules that were issued for the prevention of forest fires and for the maintenance of camp sites in a clean and sanitary condition. Also included was information about railroads, improved and unimproved

Bob Gillespie, Harvey "Harve" Dunham, Ray Dunham, and Jess Seiz's camp deer in Beaver River Country. With supper over and cookware cleaned the sportsmen relax to enjoy another evening of their fishing expedition. *Courtesy of Carolyn Browne Malkin and Robert C. Browne, Circa 1919*

roads, trails, and locations of post offices. State land along roads where travelers could camp without permits were indicated along with the locations of fire observation stations on mountain summits. Those trails were recommended as "profitable side-trips." There were even full details of a 125-mile Adirondack canoe trip from Old Forge to Saranac Lake, a paddle that is as popular today as it was in 1920.

By then the state had long established registration of the services of professional guides. The Conservation Commission inaugurated this to see to it "that no man receives his badge who is not experienced at his profession, a competent camp cook, a good boatman and familiar with his territory, its fish and its game," reported *The American Angler.*

My grandparents were avid anglers. They traveled to the mountains on their twin-cylinder Indian Scout motorcycle. Gram sat in the sidecar along with the camping and fishing gear. They did not need the assistance of a guide.

My parents became hooked on family camping from my grandparents days of following the Adirondack highways. Some of my earliest memories are the smell of the forest. I swear I began to smell balsam when I first saw the brown wooden sign along Route 28 just north of Woodgate Corners, announcing in large letters that travelers were entering the Adirondack Park. I remember sitting in cramped backseat quarters and my father announcing "Deadman's Curve" as he slowed the car to safely negotiate the sharp ninety-degree bend in the road at White Lake corners.

I remember the Chevy sedan was loaded with camping gear that first year of family camping. The trunk was stuffed full, the roof rack loaded to capacity. Packed between, around and in the foot wells on each side of the center hump below our feet were blankets, pillows, clothing, groceries and a few toys. As tucked-in as we were, however, I don't remember being a bit uncomfortable.

I also remember the cast-iron pot, kettle, and large lumberjack size griddle we used to cook over the open fire. Those and other various sized blackened cast-iron cooking paraphernalia are still part of my camping collection although I don't use them as much anymore.

Old-fashioned cast iron cookware is big and heavy, blackened and beautiful. Adirondack guides cooked with them generations ago and if seasoned correctly the cookware would be around years later to serve great grandchildren.
Courtesy Bill Zullo, Hamilton County Historian

Spam™ was a product commonly taken to Adirondack campgrounds in my childhood years. It was a popular lunch meat. It and canned Canadian bacon were part of the breakfast repast of eggs and pancakes. Although they are not there today, every time I walk by two Seventh Lake campsites where water wells stood. I remember pumping the handle to fill a bucket of water as I smelled Span cooking along with the odor of pine wood burning.

I have always been fond of sitting around a campfire. It held an unexplained allure for me as a child. I enjoyed roasting hotdogs and marshmallows on a stick as well as poking sticks into the fire, then pulling the bright poker out and whirling the glowing end in the night time air. I'll never forget the Eighth Lake campsite we were in when my friend, Gary, mistakenly bit into a crispy marshmallow. He had thought the flaming sweet treat extinguished when he blew on it, only to have it burst into flame as he put it into his mouth. His parent had a hair-raising drive from Inlet to a hospital in Utica that evening.

In time I became the family fire-tender. Today, sitting around the fire pit is as enjoyable an outdoor experience as it ever was.

Ma and Pa cooked with cast iron cookware. Imperfectly sealing lids, surface blemishes, and an oily smell are all unique and original to cast iron cookware. *Courtesy Special Collections, Feinberg Library, SUNY College at Plattsburgh*

Unidentified campers at Deerfoot Lodge on Whitaker Lake, Speculator, N.Y. After World War II, aluminum was plentiful. It seemed everything was being made out of it. Pots and pans did not escape this transition. Cast iron cookware was out of vogue. Too heavy, black instead of shiny silver and it heated and cooled quickly. (Aluminum is now being investigated as a possible cause for the increase in Alzheimer's disease.)
Courtesy Bill Zullo, Hamilton County Historian

Recipe | **CAMPGROUND APPLESAUCE-MEAT BAKE**

Campground Applesauce-Meat Bake is a flavorsome twist for using Spam™. My father was very familiar with this canned precooked meat product made by Hormel Foods Corporation. Dad said soldiers commonly referred to Spam as "Special Army Meat" based on its introduction during World War II. At the close of the war, a troupe of former servicewomen was assembled by Hormel Foods to promote Spam from coast to coast. The Hormel Girls associated the food with being patriotic. In 1948, two years after its formation, the troupe had grown to 60 women, with 16 forming an orchestra. The show went on to become a radio program whose main selling point was Spam. The Hormel Girls were disbanded in 1953.

Ingredients:

2 cups sweetened applesauce (1 one-pound can).

¼ cup brown sugar.

¼ cup chopped onion.

1 tablespoon vinegar.

1 tablespoon prepared mustard.

1 12-ounce can Spam cut in 6 or 8 slices.

1 clove garlic, minced (optional).

2 tablespoons melted butter.

1 cup soft bread crumbs.

Directions: Mix first 4 ingredients in a 10 x 6 x 1½-inch baking dish. Lightly spread mustard on the meat; arrange on applesauce. Add garlic to butter; toss with crumbs; sprinkle over meat. Bake in hot oven (400°F.) 15 minutes. Makes 3 or 4 servings.

Recipe | **RUDD'S RED & WHITE STEAK**

This was an old standby iron skillet favorite at camp, at home and in the campground. I named it after the owners of the Rudds' Red & White store in Inlet where we bought our meat when tent camping in the Fulton Chain. Mom's note reports it cost $1.79 to purchase the ingredients in 1953.

Ingredients:

3 pounds rolled. Boneless beef chuck.

1 tablespoon salt.

½ teaspoon pepper.

flour.

3 medium onions, sliced.

1 large green pepper, sliced fat

[amount is left to the cook's discreation].

19-ounce can of tomatoes.

½ teaspoon thyme.

½ teaspoon celery salt.

1 tablespoon prepared mustard.

¾ cup cooked peas.

Directions: Wipe meat with damp cloth; slice in 6 steaks. Season with salt and pepper, and dredge with flour. In skillet, cook onions and pepper in melted fat until tender. Remove from skillet. Put meat in skillet and brown on both sides, turning carefully. Top meat with onions and pepper. Add tomatoes and

Trailer camping in the Adirondack Mountains, Circa 1930s. *Author's Collection*

seasonings; cover and simmer about 1 ½ hours until meat is tender. Add peas. Makes 6 servings.

Recipe **FULTON CHAIN BEEF STEW 'N' HERB DUMPLINGS**

This was another cast iron pan recipe. Mom said it was "A solid meal with feather-light dumplings." The ingredients cost $2.00 in 1953. When camping at Eighth lake Campgrounds, we used to purchase fresh vegetables and fruit from Kalil's Grocery in Inlet.

Ingredients:

3 pounds boneless beef chuck.

flour [amount is left to the cook's discreation].

1 medium onion, chopped.

3 tablespoons fat.

1 bay leaf.

1 teaspoon celery seed.

1 tablespoon salt.

½ teaspoon pepper.

1 pound green beans, cut.

herb dumplings.

Directions: Wipe meat with damp cloth; cut in 1½-inch cubes; roll in flour. Brown with onion in fat in large, heavy kettle. Add bay leaf, celery seed, salt, pepper, and 3 cups of water; cover; simmer for 1½ hours. Add beans, and cook for 15 minutes longer, or until meat and beans are tender. If desired, thicken stew with flour mixed with a little cold water. Drop dumpling batter from tablespoon into gently boiling stew. Cover; cook for 15 minutes. Serves 6 to 8 people.

Recipe **HERB DUMPLINGS**

Ingredients:

3 cups sifted cake flour.

1¼ teaspoon baking powder.

1 teaspoon salt.

2 tablespoons shortening.

2 tablespoons chopped fresh herbs, or 2 teaspoons dried herbs, or 1 teaspoon poultry seasoning.

1 cup milk, minus 1 tablespoon.

Directions: Sift dry ingredients. Blend in shortening with fork. Add herbs and milk. Mix lightly just until flour is moistened.

The Mitchell family on their way to the Fulton Chain of Lakes. Circa 1900s.
Courtesy Roy E. Wires (The Emily Mitchell Wires Collection)

CHAPTER 40

Problem Mice and Camp Beverages

AS ADIRONDACK HERMIT Noah John Rondeau grew older and less agile, snow depth kept him close to his wilderness hermitage. Formerly long trap lines were reduced to a mere mile or so around Cold River.

As yet, snow depth has not kept me from regular visits to check Ruff 'n It I and Ruff 'n It II, my two camps. Ruff 'n It II is a modified Adirondack lean-to closer to home. I planned it that way knowing there will come a day when, like Noah, I will find it necessary to reduce the length of my snowshoe outings.

Unoccupied camps, no matter where they are, are subject to vandalism and theft. Yet, there was a time when it was unusual to find a camp locked. Woodsmen had an open-door policy. Anyone was welcome to use another's property. The only condition was that the occupant exercise reasonable care and replace all the dry tinder and firewood used.

This time-honored Adirondack tradition worked well for a long time. A lost, wet or wayward hunter, fisherman or forest traveler could find shelter and food, spending a night of comfort beside a wood-fired stove. There was little thought of stealing or destruction of camp property.

Once, it simply wasn't natural for Adirondack woodsmen to steal, but the character of the woods and mountains has changed. Even Noah found that to be true at Cold River. Right around 1944, he began to padlock his hut's door, and he stashed his most valuable items in Mammoth Graveyard, a cluster of galvanized garbage cans hidden among a collection of large boulders along a route he took to reach Ouluska Pass.

Noah's once-long winter trap lines shortened over time, but his gusto for life, his delight in gathering with old friends, and his gratitude for the foodstuff backpacked in by (Lt. to Rt.) Bess Little, Mary Dittmar and Madge Dodge helped him through the hard times. *Courtesy Dr. Adolph G. Dittmar Jr.*

I'm not naive. Those days of trust and camp doors left unlocked are gone. Nowadays, owners or caretakers of camps make periodic inspection checks throughout the year.

WHILE I haven't had many problems with human trespassers, I was not successful in constructing my retreats to be mouse-proof. As the temperature drops and snow piles high, I think the high bishop of the Knaw-It-Runabout-Us mouse clan, distinguished by his distinct high-pitched squeal, sends out the word that the camp's owner has arrived and although he's going to be firing up either the woodstove or propane heater, all four-legged inhabitants that have not been caught in traps had better scatter from their comfortable fiberglass insulation dream abode to their natural underground burrows in the subnivean zone.

Snow has a remarkable insulating nature. It traps the earth's heat. I understand with six inches or more of the white stuff, the temperature at the interface hovers around 32 degrees. This belt of lifesaving warmth is called the subnivean zone, and it supports an underground society of small mammals safe from my Victor traps, tunneling, making dens, and eating food stashes all winter long. The subnivean precinct is nature's haven for tiny mice, voles and red squirrels.

IT'S EARLY DECEMBER as I sit in camp writing this. I'm looking at the array of armed spring-loaded mouse traps. The backdrop brings back memories of Richard Smith, an old friend, who spent time during the winter in Noah Rondeau's Adirondack Mountain hermitage.

Months of isolation led the hermit to invent games to fill a void created by snowfall that kept him cabin-bound. One of his peculiar diversions had to do with making a game out of catching mice.

One rodent entertainment focused on the Town Hall Steeple Chase. As a mouse headed toward a ramp propped against a water pail, Noah declared himself the winner as the whiskered critter pitched into the water.

"No more races for him!" Noah exclaimed wryly. "It ran out of landing room."

Over the years I have also devised various ways of catching mice. My favorite is The Gauntlet.

It's nothing more than a dozen Victor spring-loaded traps laid out along one wall. I haven't figured out why they tend to favor that area. I'm inclined to believe that is where they enter the camp, but I've never been able to figure exactly where. It's almost as if this clan of mice possesses the characteristics of Rubber Man.

One time, two little Knaw-It-Runabout-Us mice ran side by side and head-to-head around the interior perimeter of the room. I sat watching, wondering which one would be the winner. Ruff 'n It's log recorded the results. "January 19, 1996. Temperature is 12°F this A.M. Ten inches of new snow fell. Two mice raced side by side; they both won The Gauntlet!"

Mice have been around to pester man as long as they have lived on earth. Mice, on the other hand, do serve to feed the predators.

Noah philosophized that in every mouse litter one is born with superior intelligence and has a natural urge to survive.

Richard tells about the day Noah devised a new method to trap mice. "He placed a chipped coffee cup scrounged from an abandoned lumber shanty upside down with the bait underneath—a dried cube of bread dipped in bacon grease. A thin twig propped the cup up on one side. When a mouse scurried under the steadied cup and began to nibble on the bait, its tail would swish against the supporting crutch, causing the cup to fall and capture the little intruder inside."

Smith said it was his habit "to pack along with my own food commodities I knew Noah would appreciate. Cocoa, sugar, dried milk, corn meal, and a dozen mousetraps which Noah called 'little back-breakers.'"

Smith's Breakfast Cocoa was a simple hot sweet drink.

On winter days he hears the sound of scampering mice,
But summer days are different.
When flowers blossom,
It's time for pluckin' and offerings to pretty girls.
Unidentified woman and Noah John Rondeau. Circa 1940s. *Author's Collection*

The Cold River hermit invented novel ways to trap mice as a form of entertainment.
Courtesy Richard J. Smith

BREAKFAST COCOA

Ingredients:

4 teaspoons of cocoa.

4 teaspoons of sugar.

⅔ cup of boiling water.

1⅓ cups of scalded milk.

Directions: Mix the cocoa and sugar, add the boiling water and let boil for 3 minutes; add the scalded milk and beat with a rotary beater just before serving.

I rarely arrived at either Ruff 'n It camp without a fresh supply of the modern models of Victor traps myself. I favor the type with the yellow plastic pan that resembles a square of Swiss cheese.

As I sit in the heated interior of the modified lean-to, leafing through the beverage section in my mother's 1933 cookbook, I'd like to believe that all the mouse occupants have moved to take advantage of the remarkable subnivean layer. I'm sipping one of Mom's especially welcome beverages, Russian Tea.

RUSSIAN TEA

Ingredients:

1 lemon.

1 orange.

¾ cup sugar or substitute.

½ teaspoon cloves in bag.

¼ cup boiling water.

1½ quarts boiling water.

3 teaspoons tea.

Directions: Squeeze fruit juices and add sugar. Steep cloves in the ¼ cup water for eight minutes. Then add that water to juice and sugar. Make tea as usual from last two items. Combine tea & spiced juices. Mom often used Tang instead of orange and sugar.

I'm guessing at least a quarter of Mom's collection of sixty-seven beverages were endorsed favorites because they were recorded in her handwriting.

Some were hot drinks, others cold. There were also warm and cold alcoholic recipes.

Mom's Irish Coffee recipe is the most splattered of all the pages. It might have been a top favorite.

Recipe **IRISH COFFEE**

Directions: One teaspoonful of brown sugar in Irish coffee mug.
Half fill the mug with black coffee.
Add one ounce of Tullamore Dew Irish Whisky
(or a whisky equally as mellow and Irish).
Stir gently until mixed.
Then add (but do not stir) a portion of whipped cream.
You then sip the Irish Coffee through the cream.
(*You should sample every one you mix.*
After you have mixed enough you'll be certain they are perfect.)

Corn muffins compliment a Cold River style fish fry. *Courtesy Dr. Adolph G. Dittmar Jr.*

The author collects snow to melt for a hot beverage. *Author's photo*

Noah John Rondeau is serving Maude Gregory. Noah is straining a steaming cup of coffee through a sieve to eliminate the grounds. Maude remembered the hermit's coffee was so strong that a spoon defied gravity and could stand upright on its own. Circa 1930s. *Photograph by Jay L. Gregory. Courtesy Dr. C.V. Latimer Jr.*

Mulled Wine was served at her parents' Camp Oasis.

Recipe **MULLED WINE**

Mulled Wine was served at my grandparent's Camp Oasis.

Ingredients: 1 cup sugar.

4 sticks cinnamon.

2 dozen whole cloves.

1 cup water.

1 lemon sliced.

Directions: Boil 5 minutes and strain. Add 4 cups hot fruit juice (orange, lemon, or pineapple). Heat but do not boil 2 quarts red wine. Combine and keep hot.

A note at the end of the directions reads: Just before serving, thrust in a red hot poker heated in the fireplace. Mom added: "I DON'T."

Grandpa's directions under "Homemade Wine" indicated: *Tie on a balloon tightly over the bottleneck. Balloon will expand & deflate-will not explode* (I hope!).

Dad's Artillery Punch indicates it makes 35–40, 5 oz. drinks. This must have been served during the years of his World War II Army day reunions.

Mom surely elevated her mother's "Syllabub," a traditional British New Year's thirst-quencher, because of what she added as a postscript to the recipe.

SYLLABUB

Recipe *Ingredients:*

2 cups white wine.

5 tablespoons grated lemon rind.

⅛ cup lemon juice.

1½ sugar.

3 cups milk.

2 cups light cream.

4 egg whites.

Nutmeg.

Directions: Combine first three ingredients. Stir in one cup of the sugar, let stand until dissolved. Combine milk and cream. Add wine mixture. Beat with rotary beater till frothy. Beat egg whites till stiff; add remaining sugar a little at a time, beating constantly until whites stand in peaks.

Pour wine mixture in punch bowl and top with puffs of egg white. Sprinkle whites with nutmeg. Makes 16 punch cups. *Syllabub is so mild that children can join in the fun.*

I don't remember if I tasted it, but reading the footnote reminded me of the offerings I enjoyed of a shot glass filled with a little bit of beer and an overflowing head of foam. It's an example of what my parents did more than six decades ago. My father was a part time-bartender. He knew the laws about giving alcohol to minors. He also knew the problems with overindulgence. My parents were responsible for their children's well-being. I know they considered the consequences to our health as well as our future attitudes toward alcohol consumption. Perhaps it's because alcohol was no mystery to me that it had little attraction later on.

I SAT FOR A FEW HOURS at the metal kitchen table, reading and making notes. My two-burner cook stove is fueled with bottled gas. Noah's stovetop consisted of a thick, flat sheet of iron placed over a halved oil drum he had partially buried in sand. It was positioned in the corner near his door as you looked out. Smith used to say, "A short-order cook could do no better. Noah always insisted on doing all the cooking my first night in camp because I had done all the snowshoeing."

Fifty years later Smith could recreate with precision what the cook surface looked like: "There spread out in a line before us was our meal to be. Little loaves of steaming corn bread, sausages, sardines, and vegetables all cooking on the hot metal surface. The can tops were still attached by a hinge and bent back for handles. That gave Noah something to hold on to as he stirred and rotated the contents, often through the blue haze of pipe smoke."

The hermit, woodsman Smith and me—we're all products of different times and yet Rondeau's and Smith's memories were reminders of a time they could never leave behind. I don't think I'll ever let go of mine either.

CHAPTER 41

Last Meal of the Season

TO AVOID a *real* spring cleaning, there were a number of things to look after when closing camp at the end of each season. Hedgehogs, chipmunks, insects, bees, raccoons, and mice were all waiting for the inexperienced or careless owner to vacate so they could move in, knock down, break, tear open, spill, trample on, and gnaw at. Chewing was what they seemed to enjoy most.

Camp owners have learned first-hand the cause-and-effect relationship of simply closing the camp door and leaving: unshuttered windows mean broken panes; unsupported beams crack or sag by spring. Sealed, vacuum-packed tin cans burst when they freeze; blankets, cloths and clothing left out are full of ragged holes by spring. Unprotected mattresses are a perfect nesting site for mice. Open crockery can be found filled with seeds, nuts and shucks; leaving a chimney uncapped is like posting a sign saying "Enter" or "Nest Here." And the calling cards of rodents—the droppings—are found scattered helter-skelter.

To combat all this, there is a standard "To Do" list when one closes for the winter:

A. Scrub away all traces of food and human salt from table, chairs, counter, and floor.
B. Leave dry food and matches in rodent-proof containers.
C. Store textiles (clothing, blankets, etc.) and bed mattresses in a tin-lined, tightly sealed can or suspend them on narrow rope from the ceiling.

D. Board up windows.

E. Keep the crawl space between floor and ground clear of bric-a-brac, and fence it off.

F. Prop sturdy poles under roof and porch beams for protection against snow and ice build-up. Arrange to have someone shovel the roof and inspect premises.

G. Disconnect water pipes, drain them, and plug the pipe ends to keep rodents out.

H. Clean woodstove and fireplace. Lay in kindling.

Bette and Jay's last camp day at North Lake. "Closing camp." The very words bring to mind a place, an atmosphere, an image of a familiar building, a covered porch where rocking and gazing, reading and telling stories took place—and the lump in the throat at having to leave it. *Photo by Wayne and Linda Cripe. Author's Collection*

During Rev. Byron-Curtiss' last ten years at camp, he grew a bit lax about following this list to the letter, and as a result Nat Foster Lodge became rundown. His last log entry departed from his usual ones, which often began, "Last night in Camp—duly and properly celebrated," and which always ended by thanking God. Instead, the eighty plus-year-old man scrawled in very shaky pen strokes, "Visited camp on this pleasant day. I desired to see it one more time before snow closes in."

"He was quiet when we turned to leave that day," Tom Kilbourn, his driver, reported, "and that was unusual for him."

The owner never returned.

Kilbourn purchased the camp from Rev. Byron-Curtiss in the fall of 1953. For the next forty years he rented the lakeside building on a yearly time-share basis.

On Bette's and my final day at Nat Foster Lodge, we left with good memories. Tom had given me all of The Reverend's log books, personal papers, and photo albums. My plan was to write about "the Bishop of North Lake." I believed a recorded knowledge of the region needed to be done and I soon wrote two books: *Adirondack Stories of the Black River Country and Under an Adirondack Influence: The Life of A. L. Byron-Curtiss 1871–1959.*

LONE PINE CAMP was a wonderful find. I accidently came on to the camp when I dropped off the steep cliffs of Mt. Tom. About halfway down, I noticed an unusual bright glint in the distance. I took a bearing and continued to descend. Without the compass bearing I would have easily lost the position for the backside of Mt. Tom was thick. Once at the camp's site, it was easy to surmise the light I saw was sunlight reflecting off the silver-coated metal roofing.

I found John Ferris's name inside. Once back home I looked up his name in the phone book and called him. John was kind. He asked how I had found it and said he'd never be going back. His weight and legs wouldn't allow it. John told me to go ahead and use the place for as long as it was there.

Earlier John Ferris's son had left this message on the back of a Mt. Tom Club posted sign inside the camp on his final day.

Propane gas is shut off, but still hooked up. Have a pot of coffee to keep
you warm. Many men have enjoyed these woods with their families;
for this we thank God. For this is God's Country. I thank all of the men
that showed me the way. Thank you for these last few weeks.

—J. Dennis Ferris

John never told me why his son abandoned the cabin. I surmised it had to
do with a lack of hunting partners, an inability to bushwhack the rough
Mt. Tom woodland any longer, his health, or the fact that the state was in
the process of purchasing the property. Maybe it was a combination of all.
There were quite a few sentimental-value articles his son and he had left
in the camp. I promised I would bring them all out for him—and I made
good on that promise.

Closing Lone Pine Camp's door for the last time must have been difficult for Dennis. It was for me, because I knew that when I returned to the
spot, all I would find would be the ashes of the building. The state was to
take ownership of the property during the late winter. As a non-conforming
structure, the building would be razed before the spring snow melted. The
normal "closing camp" routine was unnecessary this time.

I imagined Dennis lingered on his last day. I did the same thing. Alone,
I cooked an easy-to-prepare parting meal. I called it "Lone Pine Baked Mac
& Cheese with Broccoli."

Recipe | **LONE PINE BAKED MAC & CHEESE WITH BROCCOLI**

Ingredients:
2 cups uncooked elbow macaroni.
1 cup broccoli florets (fresh or frozen).
5 tablespoons butter.
2 tablespoons flour.
2 cups milk.
½ teaspoon salt.
8 ounces cheddar cheese cut into ½-inch pieces.
½ cup dry bread crumbs.
Directions: Cook macaroni, adding broccoli during the last four
minutes of cooking time. Drain. Melt 4 tablespoons butter, stir

in flour. Cook over heat, stirring for about 1 minute until it bubbles and looks smooth. Add milk and salt. Cook until sauce thickens. Add cooked macaroni, broccoli and cheese. Stir until the cheese melts. Spoon into an ungreased 2-quart casserole. Melt remaining butter. Mix bread crumbs over the macaroni and cheese. Bake 20-25 minutes at 350°F. until golden brown.

Lt. to Rt. Bill "Pete" Burdict, Phil Mair, George Mair, John Ferris. Members of the Mt. Tom Hunting Club prepare supper in Lone Pine Camp's kitchen. *Courtesy John Ferris*

"Late June 2003. I returned to the former site of Lone Pine Camp. The charred remains of the camp's gas stove still contained my sealed 'historic tube.' Should anyone ever come across the camp they will learn something about what was once here." —Jay O'Hern

Judging the length of daylight I had available following my meal, I fiddled around doing little things, not really wanting to leave but knowing I would need to soon. I didn't want to get caught after dark snowshoeing through the thick cover in the Red River Valley section of my outgoing path.

As planned, I did return the following summer. And, just as I thought, the camp had been burned. I opened the door of the charred oven and placed inside a capped PVC tube I had made up. It serves as a historical capsule. Inside I had placed some coins, a note telling a bit about what the ruins used to be, and my address. I hope that whomever might come across the old remains will write me of their find.

In the succeeding decades, wild brambles have completely covered the burn area. I doubt anyone will ever chance onto it.

Lone Pine Camp. Winter 1987

EPILOGUE

ALL THE RASCALLY Adirondack camp owners I've known are gone. In some cases not a single member of their immediate family is left alive. The old camps are leveled or owned by other families.

When I sort through my collection of camp snapshots or prepare a main meal or eat a favorite sweet, I like to think the experience continues a connection with those old places and people, where campers sunbathed on the beach, hunted and fished, and when sleepy vacationers listened to the call of loons as they snuggled in bed sheltered by beloved digs.

Those images of days gone by are meant to evoke nostalgia and summon thoughts of an earlier era in the Adirondacks when steamboats and railroads were still in use, when gasoline for a 'tin lizzy' cost only 15.3¢ a gallon,

Fulton Chain guests at Beckers, Circa 1907. *Courtesy Freda B. Westfall*

On days when work was caught up, the fiddle filled the air with sweet ole time mountain music. *Courtesy of the Piseco Historical Society*

and when winding mountain roads were rough, muddy or gravel-packed, making an automobile trip an adventure in itself. Those travelers could buy a loaf of bread for a nickle, and dinner for a dollar.

There are any number of popular social media 'Looking Back' sites that have the tendency to look through rose-colored glasses at 'the good old days,' but that isn't necessarily true. The saying is just a cilché.

Old snapshots show a lot of good times, family and friend times, and days that will never be forgotten, as long as loved ones have left us with those memories and vintage family photos are preserved in books such as in *Spring Trout and Strawberry Pancakes*, where they can be cherished.

Gone are the days we think of as "olden," yes, but good ones are also yet to come. Memories of today will parallel those of past times in many ways. And we will look back and wonder—

> *Time, oh time.*
> *Where did you go?*
> *Time oh good, good time.*
> *Where did you go?*

To those who camp, ply Adirondack waters, enjoy invigorating forest hikes, or appreciate a relaxing holiday of refreshing views—perhaps the echoes of those whose stories and recipes are shared here will enrich your Adirondack experience as well as delight your palate.🐟

A journey through the Adirondacks can be a voyage of discovery.
Courtesy of the Town of Webb Historical Association, P4669

Eagle Bay garage. *Courtesy of the Town of Webb Historical Association, P7214*

Home of the $1.00 Special. Early Adirondack diner in Eagle Bay, New York.
Courtesy of the Town of Webb Historical Association, P7195

Classmates out on a mid-summer day frolic to Nick's Lake.
Courtesy of the Town of Webb Historical Association, P2523

The early mountain camps have been converted, but continue to shelter and provide joy to a new group of owners. *Courtesy of the Town of Webb Historical Association, P2523*

Spring Trout & Strawberry Pancakes: Borrowed Tales, Quirky Cures, Camp Recipes

Today's society better understands humane treatment of animals. In 1919 it was still typical to find young baby black bears led around on a neck chain for the amusement of tourists. *Courtesy of the Piseco Historical Society*

Picnic clowns compete in a pie-eating contest. *Courtesy of the Town of Webb Historical Association, P3328*

Winter activities continue to be as popular as ever. Boys making a snowman at Piseco Lake. *Courtesy of the Piseco Historical Society*

Spring Trout & Strawberry Pancakes: Borrowed Tales, Quirky Cures, Camp Recipes

Ice fisherman. *Courtesy of the Town of Webb Historical Association, P5734*

Typical Adirondack platform tent that my grandparents could rent on state-owned land in 1938. *Author's Collection*

Breakfast in the mountains. 1922. *Courtesy of Leigh Portner*

Dad was often the chief-cook-and-bottle washer in camp. *Courtesy of Leigh Portner*

Opposite bottom: Off to experience peace and solitude in the wilds of nature.
Courtesy of John Chamberlain

Mountain climbing has continued to be a popular activity. *Courtesy of John Chamberlain*

"Fly-Trap Inn." Adirondack summits often had open-log camps back in the day. This lean-to was on top of Blue Mountain in 1918. *Courtesy of Leigh Portner*

Opposite: Typical climbing attire in the early 1900s. *Courtesy of Leigh Portner*

"Mabel the Bathing Girl in the central Adirondacks." 1920. *Courtesy of Leigh Portner*

Opposite: Good times in the Adirondack Mountains. "We met at camp and have remained friends forever." Camp Fulton Dock, Fourth Lake, 1919. *Courtesy of Leigh Portner* Inset: This billboard invited guests not only to the hotel and cottages, but also for some refreshment in the Tap Room. *Courtesy of the Town of Webb Historical Association, P4567*

COTTAGES — TAP ROOM

The Fulton HOTEL

FOURTH LAKE

6 MI. NORTH OF OLD FORGE

"The Moose River Girls." Clara, Marion, and Mabel Quackenbush. 1921.
Courtesy of Leigh Portner

Opposite top: "Competition diving with my friends was one of my fondest joys." —John Chamberlain, circa 1900s. *Courtesy of John Chamberlain*

Opposite bottom: Following the road into the mountains was an adventure in itself. Flat tires were common "Uncle Will Buell, Mother and Father fixing tire." July 28, 1919. *Courtesy of Leigh Portner*

"Walked over to Sixth Lake. Traveled by motorboat through Sixth and Seventh Lakes. Walked about a mile from Seventh to Eighth Lake. Saw an eagle's nest in the top of a tall pine tree and saw the eagle and her young. Saw the tallest and largest trees in the Adirondacks, also beaver dams and houses. Came back at 5 P.M." —LeNora Mae Quackenbush, July 24, 1920. *Courtesy of Leigh Portner*

"Started for the Adirondacks at 5 A.M. Camped on Graham's property. The boys slept in a tent and we girls slept in the shack. Walked to Inlet, climbed Rocky (Point) Mt. and had a frankfurter roast out on the sand point. An encampment of *gypsies* were over in the woods a little north of us. I felt a little afraid of them. A very full day." —LeNora Mae Quackenbush, August 5, 1920. *Courtesy of Leigh Portner*

"Drove over to Camp Fulton. Walked the Bald Mt. Trail and climbed the mt. Ate our lunch there. Went bathing in Fourth Lake and to the movies in evening." —LeNora Mae Quackenbush, August 10, 1926. *Courtesy of Leigh Portner*

Mabel and Leigh are delayed by a smashup with Ernest's Dodge car. To avoid hitting an on-coming car on their side of the road, he took to the ditch. Happened 10 miles below Old Forge. Quite a bit of damage done and a problem to get it repaired." —LeNora Mae Quackenbush, August 7, 1920. *Courtesy of Leigh Portner*

Time, oh time. Where did you go?
Time oh good, good time. Where did you go?
Margery Hubbard, Alice Hummel, Sue Eatlore, Reba__, Fulton Chain, 1918.
Courtesy of Leigh Portner

The day's fun at Golden Beach at Raquette Lake compared to a ground breaking event. "Big news. The papers are full of praise for the American aviator, Charles Lindbergh, who is the first to accomplish a nonstop flight from N.Y. to Paris."
—Helen Barton, May 21, 1927. *Courtesy of Marilyn Breakey*

Old Recipes Call for Can Sizes

THIS CONVERSION CHART is helpful when presented with a recipe that that calls for a "No. 303 can of fruit cocktail."

Can Size	Volume of Food	Weight of Food
No. 1	1+¼ cups	10+½–12 oz.
No. 300	1+¾ cups	14–16 oz.
No. 303	2 cups	16–17 oz.
No. 2	2+½ cups	20 oz.
No. 2+½	3+½ cups	27–29 oz.
No. 3	5+¾ cups	51 oz.
No. 10	3 quarts	6+½ lb.–7 lb.; 5 oz.

A Trip to the North Woods, 1954

By Mary Lovejoy Thomas

While this story recalls a seven-year-old's family trip to northern Ontario, the author notes that the family also camped several times in the Adirondacks, and she has since learned that the two regions have much in common. Early on, both areas were heavily logged and trapped, and few old-growth trees remain in either. Fortunately, the land surrounding the large Canadian lake so dear to the author's heart—with the exception of privately-owned parcels grandfathered in—is now a roadless Provincial Park and enjoys many of the protections that the Forever Wild act affords the Adirondack Park. The two areas share natural beauty, cold lakes and wild rushing rivers, good fishing and hunting, frequent wildlife sightings, and the collective joy of all whose favorite direction is due north, until civilization falls away and its clamor is replaced by contented sighs.

THE DAY BEFORE we left for the north woods was almost as good as the day before Christmas. We drove for two long days from Cleveland in our old Nash Ambassador, camping overnight somewhere in northern Michigan the first night, then continuing the next day to the ferries that crossed the Straits of Mackinac and the St. Mary's River, then into the woods.

There were no expressways or turnpikes in the 1950s, and that made the trip more interesting for my brother and me. There were always things we found hysterical—decrepit buildings with faded "EAT" signs cracked us up for some reason, and we'd pass the time playing the alphabet game, where we'd look for a sign that started with an A and then a B and so forth. If I tried to explain this to my granddaughter, she would probably ask, "Why didn't you just watch DVDs?" I'm glad we didn't. We wouldn't have been able to hear our dad jokingly singing "Tenting Tonight On the Old Campground" or our favorite:

Gentlemen will please refrain
From flushing toilets while the train
Is standing in the station,
I love you.

I'm sure the last line was ad-libbed. He and Mother always looked fondly at one another when he sang it, and she shook her head and said, "Oh, Jack!"

We'd sigh blissfully when Mother announced, "It's time to start looking for a roadside table." In those days, picnic tables in little clearings along country roads were common. There are still a few on Route 23 along Lake Huron. To John and me, the words "roadside table" also meant we'd stop at the next gas station for soda pop—something we were rarely allowed to have. It came out of a big red cooler full of ice, and the thick glass bottles could not have held more than 7 ounces of sweet fizzy pop, but that was heaven enough for us.

Our picnic lunch menu never varied. Mother always used up the last of the eggs we had at home and made egg salad sandwiches on bread she baked herself, probably to use up the last of the milk. There would be potato chips, another rare treat, and homemade oatmeal cookies. It all tasted perfect in the cool maple shade, with the thrill of seeing the big lake not far off.

Making camp was a big chore for a 1950s family. Our tent was heavy waxed canvas, the poles and pegs wood. It took some doing to get it up with any degree of certainty that it would stay up. While John and Daddy saw to that, Mother and I scouted the campground for firewood and raspberry and blueberry bushes. Not many families considered camping "a vacation" back then, and there always seemed to be plenty of both wood and berries.

Back at camp, Mother would start waving around the can of potted meat, taunting my father. "You know why I brought this, of course! You know what this means if you don't catch any fish!"

It was a long-standing joke. After four years on a Navy ship in World War II, Daddy had seen enough potted meat to last him a lifetime. It was something that was never served at our house. I think we brought the same can with us on our trips north for a decade. We always caught fish, and I never did find out how that potted meat tasted.

There was no time to fish that first night, even though Lake Huron was mere footsteps from camp, so we almost always had canned beef stew topped with Bisquick® dumplings. It was cooked in a Dutch oven on a folding grate over the campfire, and we didn't get around to eating until it was dark and the stars were beginning to pop out. In fact, the stars were our entertainment as we toasted marshmallows and Daddy pointed out constellations and told us some of the old legends about how they got their names.

What would we have done without Bisquick®? It was a camp staple and made quick work of the next morning's blueberry pancakes. I suppose the canned orange juice we drank was sour compared to today's refrigerated ones, but it tasted fine to us in the damp cool dawn.

By the time we got to Mackinaw City, it was noon, and time for a treat: whitefish sandwiches at a restaurant that overlooked the wide stretch of water we would soon cross. I remember the first time my mother told me we would take a ferry boat across the Straits, and that Daddy would drive the car onto the boat. I pictured Tinkerbell perched on the bow of a wooden rowboat, and our great hulking Nash filling the boat completely. If that was how it was going to be, I trusted completely in Tinkerbell's ability to get us to the other side of the turquoise water.

Of course, the ferry was a huge steel ship that held dozens of cars on the bottom deck and moved oh-so-slowly to St. Ignace on the other side, while we hung over the railing on the upper deck, straining northward, willing speed.

"We're really up north now," my dad would say elatedly as he drove the Nash off the ferry with a bump. It took a little over an hour to cross Michigan's Upper Peninsula, a wilderness of nothing but trees and road. While Daddy drove, Mother would school us sternly on what to say to the customs officer in Canada. We were not supposed to goof around and say we were citizens of Krypton, for example, or that the purpose of our visit to Canada was to join Sergeant Preston and the Mounties. Once we got across the St. Mary's on another ferry, the moment of truth came. I always held my breath and waited for the Big Questions. Invariably, the customs officer ignored me completely, had a short friendly chat with my dad, and waved us on, wishing us a good holiday.

After a stop in Sault Ste. Marie for a quick supper and a trip to the grocery store, it was nearly dark by the time we arrived at the camp. The dirt road in was so rough that in some places boulders almost scraped the bottom of the car. It was an excruciatingly slow five miles off the main road, which itself was termed "improved" because it was graded gravel for 90 miles from the Soo.

Then, at the top of the last hill, we'd see the glimmer of the lake through the trees—navy blue, sparkling in the moonlight, vast and miraculous. Our beloved lake. Our simple cottage. As darkness and the evening chill came on, we stashed our groceries and gear and Mother got a fire going in the wood kitchen stove while John and I fetched pails of water from the lake and Daddy manhandled a chunk of block ice, purchased at the Last Chance Trading Post, into the icebox. The kerosene lamps were lit, and there was time for one game of rummy before we blew out the lamps and went to bed, listening to loons calling across the lake as we drifted off.

The next day, Daddy spoke to a few other cottagers to find out what the fish were biting on. Sometimes it was nightcrawlers, sometimes minnows. Lake trout, the big lunking denizens of the deep, went for lures. Mother and Daddy went lake trout fishing early in the morning. Mother ran the motor while Daddy pulled on the huge pole with its heavy steel line. He often brought in one fish big enough to feed all four of us for several days—the meat a lovely pink-orange, juicy and sweet, fried in butter in a cast iron skillet. We always had mashed potatoes with the fish. Mother said it would cushion the bones if we happened to swallow any. Sliced beefsteak tomatoes and wild blueberry pie balanced the meal perfectly.

After dinner, it was bass fishing time. It was best just offshore in about twenty feet of water. Equipped with the recommended bait and red-and-white bobbers, my brother and I lowered our lines until we felt the sinkers hit bottom, then pulled them up a few rounds, picturing how appealing our bait must look to the small-mouth bass whose shadows we could see moving in the clear water below the boat. We could feel them and even see them nosing and nibbling down there. Then finally, a good hard tug and we knew, fish on. Fish for breakfast!

"The Best Way to Prepare Fish" was a frequent topic of conversation among the handful of cottagers at the lake. There were those who said they should be simply gutted, scaled, dipped in cornmeal and fried in whatever grease was handy. Way on the other side were those who skinned, deboned and filleted the fish before they even thought about cooking them. We fell somewhere in the middle. If a lake trout was especially huge—say ten pounds—Daddy would just behead and gut it, take off the fins, scale it, and cut it crosswise into steaks about an inch thick. Mother would soak the steaks in milk for a bit, then dip them in seasoned biscuit mix or flour and fry them in butter. We quickly learned how to lift the delicious flesh away from the bone.

For some reason, bass were cooked differently. They were gutted and thoroughly scaled, and then went through a three-dip process—flour, milk and egg, and cornmeal. Then into the pan, which contained half melted butter and half vegetable shortening. Some people deep-fried them, but we used about an inch of cooking fat in the pan and turned the fish once. In any case, fish were always fried until they had a brown, crispy crust. No one ever thought to bake them in the oven of the wood stove or season them with Cajun spices. The ubiquitous barbecue grill was still in the future.

Even today, there are no more than two dozen cabins on the whole lake—one that would be surrounded by hundreds of residences if most of it had not long ago been declared a Provincial Park—with no road leading to it.

The lake is too vast and deep and cold to be much affected by a few hundred humans visiting for a short time each year. In this part of the north woods, nature is in charge, and there is something wonderfully comforting in one's own insignificance.

Recipe　**FRUIT CRISP**

When you're far away from the nearest store, you get creative with what you have on hand. This crisp can be made with raspberries, blueberries, apples or a combination of these. If we were low on sugar, we added raisins for sweetening.

3 cups fruit.

1 cup sugar (brown sugar if you have it, or ½ white and ½ brown).

⅔ cup flour or biscuit mix.

⅔ cup oatmeal.

1 teaspoon cinnamon.

1 egg.

5 TB. melted butter.

Directions: Grease an 8 x 8 pan or something close. Pour in the fruit. Combine the flour, oatmeal, sugar, cinnamon and egg and sprinkle over the fruit. Drizzle evenly with melted butter. Bake at 400°F. about 30 minutes.

At a wilderness cabin, the only way to have ice cream was to make it ourselves. Instead, we poured the cream off the top of the un-homogenized milk that came in bottles and saved it for a few days until we had enough to top a dessert like this one with it. We didn't whip it, either.

These days, I'd opt for vanilla ice cream.

PORCUPINES WERE the bane of our dogs' existence when we camped in the northwoods. I remember waking up more than one morning to a muzzle full of quills and a pleading expression that needed no translation: Help! The only solution was a long trip to the nearest town where a vet could be found. The dog was anesthetized and the quills were pulled all the way through its poor lips, coming out the inside of its mouth. One would think one application of porcupine would be a lifetime lesson. It wasn't the case with any of our dogs. In fact, they seemed to be more determined than ever to "get" that creature who had made them so miserable!

Recipe | ADELLA LOVEJOY HULL'S PORCUPINE MEATBALLS

Ingredients:

1 lb. lean ground beef

½ cup uncooked white rice

2 tsp. minced onion, or more to taste

1 tsp. salt

1 beaten egg

28 oz. can of diced tomatoes with basil, garlic and oregano

Directions: Put the tomatoes in a large, deep frying pan. Mix meat, rice, onion, salt and egg. Form into 1" balls and arrange in the frying pan over the tomatoes. Bring to a boil; then simmer gently about an hour. As they cook, the rice swells and sticks out for the porcupine effect. 🍴

"Getting ready to face a chilly day at Lake Eaton campground while my little dog Donny waits for me to get the show on the road. Mother and I slept in the car, an old Nash whose seats folded down. We were lucky we could turn the heater on every now and then at night. My brother and dad slept in the waxed canvas tent."
—Mary L. Dennis. *Courtesy Mary L. Dennis*

APPENDIX C

"Clean Eating" in the Adirondacks

TERRY AND GEORGE CATALDO's Independence Camp takes its name from the Independence River that runs through their North Country property. As we sat together, we ate raspberry-rhubarb pie and talked about recipes and how meal preparation has changed. In 2015, the couple was in their mid-eighties. I'll call George a logger, although he has worked in every aspect of the lumber business except as a river driver. "Oh how I loved the breakfasts in those old lumber camps," he recalled with a gleam in his eye. He described eating piles of pork chops, pies, and seemingly anything under the sun for breakfast. "Those were the days."

Terry also enjoyed remembering.My mention of the depth of the mid-March snow and the long driveway they needed to clear to reach the main road reminded her of the school sleigh bus that transported her to school. I'd never heard of one.

Terry described it as homemade on a sleigh body. She said, "Andrew Seelman built the box with pine lumber, installing a Model T windshield and a small opening for the horse's reins to pass inside the 'bus.' Entrance was through a door in the back. The passengers sat on fixed benches on each side." There was no heater. On the coldest days, Terry said, "Mrs. Seelman warmed soap stones to help keep the bus warm."

If the "bus" happened to arrive at the one-room school house before the teacher, the children would gather at the nearest farm. We "were usually entertained by Pat O'Brien and his half-brother, Alton Longway, who often had a wild animal, like a fox or bobcat, in a huge outdoor cage," Terry recalled. "If it was extremely cold we would go in the barn. One time I remember riding home from school and dozing off, as was easy to do in the slow moving vehicle. We went over a bump and the sleigh bus tipped over. Out we climbed, righted the bus and got back in again, continuing on home. No one was hurt, just surprised."

I had heard stories from my mother about her childhood school day experiences and later, her early days of teaching. She often used the term 'scholar' in place of 'student' when she spoke about her classroom children. What was even stranger was that when the first school cafeteria opened, allowing children a hot meal prepared by cafeteria cooks, their classroom mother sat with her scholars during the dinner period and saw to it that each and every boy and girl ate everything that was placed on their dinner tray. She would be shocked to see how today's school foods and cafeteria ways have changed.

Terry was younger than my mother by fifteen years, but many of her experiences were similar to Mom's. Children carried their dinner to school. Though some children lived close enough to go home to eat, the majority preferred eating at school, mainly so they could play for the remainder of the noon hour break. Mother mentioned hard-boiled eggs were a staple that nested in every child's dinner pail, along with sandwiches of bread, butter, and jelly. Then there was also cold ham or sausage, or dried beef (known as chipped to me). Also certain to be included in a dinner pail were cheese, an apple, a pear, or a bunch of grapes when they were available. The most anticipated portion of a meal was the sugary treats: the cookies (molasses, sugar, raisin-infused sugar), a slice of pie, or some sort of sweet roll.

Terry said she didn't carry a dinner pail.

"I used recycled paper sacks to carry a sandwich, fruit and a cookie to school. In the winter, all the mothers took turns providing a hot lunch. My mother would make a large batch of vegetable-beef soup.

"The dish was kept hot on the wood stove, which was used to heat the school. "My favorite hot lunch was when the school marm instructed us to bring a scrubbed potato, in which we were to carve our initials. On arrival at school, we would place our potato in the oven on top of the stove. By lunchtime the potatoes were done and the teacher would place each potato in a soup bowl, cut them in half and smother them in butter. Then we'd add a bit of salt, dig in and pop each spoonful into our mouths. The skin was the best part.

Terry and George Cataldo, January 28, 2013. *Courtesy of Theresa Z. Cataldo*

Pat O'Brien contributed stories in the lumber camp section of my *Flapjacks for Lumberjacks: Stories, Memories, and Recipes from Adirondack and Tug Hill Lumber Camps* cook book. Had he known Terry had remembered his frisky antics he might have rolled off more about his school day clowning around other than how he used to crack his hard-boiled egg in a single blow against his forehead—a skill no one could match as well, no matter how much they tried.

Terry continued: "During World War II the government provided us with surplus pork and beans and split pea soup, so that the mothers no longer brought hot lunches. What a blow! The teacher would watch to make sure that I would eat them. After a bite or two she would concentrate on her own lunch; then my friend Kitty would eat a bite of hers and then reach over and take a bite of mine. That is friendship! To this day I do not eat those foods."

A younger generation might view Terry and George as old-time folks, based on their ages and backgrounds. While their childhoods might seem like "the good ol' days," their exercise routine, lifestyle, cooking and eating habits today are cutting-edge. There are no hot cross buns with delicious sugary icing drizzled over the top baking in Terry's wood-fired kitchen oven.

Terry's recipes call for "health food" ingredients—foods that are not processed. They choose to cook differently than mainstream America. They do not eat meat. A majority of their food is raised in their own vegetable garden. It's a choice Terry accepted as a challenge following triple bypass surgery and a diagnosis of inherited diabetes. She took Level I and II classes on the macrobiotic lifestyle and cooking at the Kushi Institute in Becket, Massachusetts, and says the classes changed her life.

Today's Adirondackers are as much in touch with the outside world as everyone else, connected by the Internet, print media, and television. Like

Brantingham Lake Inn located in Lewis County was a popular wilderness hostelry in the western Adirondacks east of Route 12. *From a Beach postcard. Courtesy of George Cataldo*

Terry and George Cataldo, they know that a diet laden with sugar and "bad" fats is not healthy, and there is a trend toward "clean eating"—avoiding anything processed and trying to eat organically whenever possible. Terry's recipes are wholly in line with this trend, and the couple's robust health is testimony to its effectiveness.

| Recipe | **TERRY'S PIE CRUST**[10] (Makes 2 large Crusts) |

By Theresa Z. Cataldo

Terry recommends King Arthur flour.

Ingredients:

Place in a large bowl:

3 cups white whole wheat flour.

Mix together and shake in a quart jar:

½ teaspoon sea salt.

4 tablespoons applesauce.

Add and shake again:

½ cup Extra Virgin Olive Oil.

½ cup water.

Directions: Stir liquids into the dry ingredients. [*Some flour is drier than others; add a bit more water if needed.*] Sift a bit of flour onto counter and over rolling pin. After rolling pie crust, it may help to lift the crust over the rolling pin. [*This crust will not be as flaky as when made with lard or shortening, but it is healthier.*] *Pie baking hint: To sweeten fruit that is placed in the pie crust, use Barley Malt, Rice Syrup, frozen concentrated juice, or cranberry juice.*

| Recipe | **BAKED OATMEAL** |

By Theresa Z. Cataldo

Terry reports: My Baked Oatmeal is like bar cookies. Place the batter in a rectangular pan or for a thinner snack use a sided cookie sheet.

Directions: Soak in a large bowl 2½ cups rolled oats and 1 ½ or 1¾ cups skimmed milk or fruit juice.

In a smaller bowl mix together ½ cup olive or other veggie oil, ½ cup barley malt or other natural sweetener, 3 large eggs, and 2 teaspoons vanilla extract.

Toss and mix with oatmeal mixture: 2 teaspoons cinnamon and ½ teaspoon ginger, 1½ cups quick oats, 2 teaspoons baking powder, and ¼ teaspoon sea salt (1 large pinch).

[*Cooking hint: 1 rounded cup of fresh, frozen, or dried fruit may be added and mixed together. This mixture should be quite moist. Add more liquid if needed.*]

Place in greased 9 in. X 13 in. pan. Bake at 350°F. for 40–45 minutes. Toothpick should come out dry.

Recipe **CRUCIFEROUS SALAD**

By Theresa Z. Cataldo

This salad has all the currently healthy things in it.

Directions: Shred cabbage, broccoli, cauliflower and kale or any other greens like spinach, mustard greens (small amount), chard, etc. Add a few green onions or any mild onion and a red pepper for color. I use my Pampered Chef shredder for the first 3 veggies and my macro knife to slice other veggies finely. Parsley is also a nice addition if you lack green veggies. When veggies are cut, sprinkle ½ teaspoon (more if making a large salad) of sea salt over veggies. Stir and then press in bowl with weight for at least an hour. Taste and drain in colander. If too salty rinse in cold water. Thoroughly drain and add a few table-spoons of Italian dressing. Garnish with red pepper and pars-ley. Serve to hungry people. —Amen, Terry.

Recipe **SQUASHAGE (VEGETARIAN SAUSAGE)**

By Theresa Z. Cataldo

Gardeners can't wait to make this great recipe when there is a bumper crop of zucchini. Terry said she invented this recipe because she "missed the sausage my mother used."

Directions: Cut very large zucchini squash in quarters length-wise; remove and discard the seeds. Grate the squash on a coarse grater into a large bowl; sprinkle about ½ to ¾ teaspoon of sea salt over squash; stir. Place a plate, smaller than the bowl, on top, then put on a weight. (A washed rock, a quart jar of water, or a #10 can works well.) After ½ hours, drain most of the liquid off the squash. Add 2 beaten eggs. Sprinkle a little pepper, ½ to 1 teaspoon sage, and 1 teaspoon ground nettles (if you would like), 1 or 2 cups of quick cooking oatmeal (not instant) and mix thoroughly. This mixture should be somewhat moist. Let stand for a few minutes. Heat griddle to 350°F. Drop patties on lightly greased griddle and flatten with spatula (press down with a potato masher to about ½ inch think). It takes 10-15 minutes to a side. Good hot with veggies, brown rice and a salad. Makes a great sandwich with plain yogurt, pickles and or lettuce and tomato.

Terry footnoted: "I found that the Quick Oats absorbs the liquid much quicker." She often leaves them out.

Recipe **ENERGY BARS**

By Theresa Z. Cataldo

A great item to take on the trail!

Mix together in a large bowl:

2 cups chopped pecans, almonds, walnuts.

1 cup of date pieces and raisins.

1 cup cut apricot pieces.

4 tablespoons spelt[11] or unbleached flour.

¼ cup of oatmeal (not instant).

2 tablespoons ground flax.

¼ teaspoon baking powder.

¼ teaspoon sea salt.

Whisk together and add to dry ingredients.

Stir or use hands as needed:

1 large egg.

3 tablespoons barley malt.

2 tablespoons olive oil.

1 teaspoon vanilla.

Place in square, lightly greased pan.

Bake 20–25 minutes at 325°F. until golden brown.

Cool 5 minutes and cut into squares.

BANANA BREAD COOKIES

By Theresa Z. Cataldo

Not only does this recipe sound wonderful; the cookies taste terrific.

Mix dry ingredients together:

2 cups whole wheat flour

1 teaspoon baking powder and 1 teaspoon baking soda

1 three finger pinch of sea salt

1 cup chopped pecans or walnuts

Mix liquids together:

3 mashed ripe bananas

2 beaten eggs

¾ cups barley malt (or ½ cup molasses and ¼ cup brown sugar)

½ cup olive oil

1 teaspoon vanilla

Stir liquids into dry ingredients.

Test the consistency of the dough by dropping a spoonful on a small greased pan. Bake at 350° F. for 8 to 11 minutes. Cool on rack. Depending on scoop size, makes about 28 cookies.

BARLEY CABBAGE CASSEROLE (large size)

By Theresa Z. Cataldo

This can be likened to a kind of vegan Shepard's Pie

Cook together 1 cup barley and 5 cups boiling water and ½ teaspoon sea salt. Cut in bite size pieces and sauté together in small amount of oil: ½ medium head cabbage, 6–8 medium size carrots, and 2 large onions. Reconstitute 1 cup texturized vegetable protein with one cup water and season with Kitchen Bouquet and soy sauce. Sauté until brown. Measure ¾ cup whole wheat croutons. In a well-oiled dish, place ingredients in layers (barley, vegetables, TVP and croutons) or they may be mixed together. Sprinkle 1 or 2 tablespoons of Umeboshi vinegar over casserole. Bake 20 minutes at 350°F. (I just do mine on top of a wood stove.)

Terry and George Cataldo live close to the site of the once well-known Brantingham Lake Inn, where friendly waitresses added to diners' pleasure. *Courtesy of George Cataldo*

Recipe **GRANOLA**

By Theresa Z. Cataldo

This is a great way to control the sugar and fat in granola.

Mix together dry ingredients in large dishpan:

8 to 10 cups old fashioned oatmeal

1 to 2 cups wheat, oat or rice bran

1 cup ground flax

1 to 2 cups sunflower seeds

1 to 2 cups chopped nuts (optional)

1 to 2 cups raisins, figs, etc.

Blenderize ingredients:

2 plus cups warm water or juice

3 or 4 ripe bananas, apples or fully ripe fruit

1½ cups barley malt, rice syrup, honey, or black strap molasses

Combine and mix all ingredients with a large spoon. Place on 2 large cookie sheets and bake at 300°F. until golden brown. Turn with spatula and continue baking 15–20 minutes or until slightly dry. You may cut recipe in half.

Recipe **SWEET AND SOUR LENTILS**

By Theresa Z. Cataldo

It's claimed that ½ cup of lentils twice a week
can lower cholesterol dramatically.

1 cup lentils

2 cups water

1 bay leaf

½ teaspoon sea salt

Bring to a boil and simmer 20 minutes. Test for doneness

Add:

¼ cup apple or pineapple juice

¼ cup vinegar

1 clove garlic crushed

⅛ teaspoon ground cloves

Heat until bubbly.

Serve over brown rice. Serves 6-8 adults. Good warmed up.

Lake Brantingham Inn, N.Y. kitchen staff. August 15, 1956.
Hard's Photographic Service, Lowville, N.Y. Courtesy of George Cataldo

BEST-EVER MUFFIN OR DROP COOKIES

By Theresa Z. Cataldo

Mix together in large bowl:

1 cup whole wheat pastry flour

1 cup wheat germ or ground flax

¾ cup sunflower seeds

½ cup wheat or oat bran

1 tablespoon baking powder

½ teaspoon sea salt

1 teaspoon cinnamon

In a small bowl mix together:

1 cup finely grated carrots

¾ cup golden raisins

2 eggs and ½ cup water

¼ cup barley malt or honey

¼ cup black strap molasses

¼ cup olive oil

1 teaspoon vanilla extract

Oil pans and either make into drop cookies or muffins.

Bake at 350°F. Muffins need about 20 minutes of baking; cookies about 10+ minutes.

Makes about a dozen muffins or two dozen cookies.

FOOTNOTES

1. *Under an Adirondack Influence: The Life of A. L. Byron-Curtiss 1871–1959*, The Forager Press, 2008. (pg. 3)

2. The "State House" in Atwell, N.Y. was the residence provided to the Gatekeeper of the North Lake Reservoir and his family by the State of New York. (pg. 13)

3. The Black River flood occurred in the Black River Valley on April 21 and 22, 1869, causing damage amounting to $800,000. (pg. 15)

4. *Adirondack Stories of the Black River Country*, North Country Books, 2003. (pg. 27)

5. Felons are closed-space infections of the fingertip pulp. (pg. 83)

6. A salt spoon is an old fashion term. It refers to a miniature utensil used with an open salt cellar. The items were used from a time before table salt was free-flowing. (pg. 84)

7. "A Neophyte in Hermit Country: Trial by Bushwhack," by William J. O'Hern. *Adirondack Peak Experiences: Mountaineering Adventures, Misadventures, and the Pursuit of "The 46."* 2009. Compiled and Edited by Carol Stone White. (pg. 128)

8. 2 cups. See Appendix B. (pg. 129)

9. Further reading about fires in the Adirondacks can be found in "Inferno in the Adirondacks," by Harry W. Hicks, found in *Adirondack Kaleidoscope and North Country Characters*, 2013. (pg. 227)

10. Historical side bar: Some people prefer to eat only the inside of a piece of pie—the custard or fruit—and never touch the crust because they believe it is unwholesome due to lard or unhealthy shortening. I am one of those people who leaves the crust on the plate. I'm afraid the evidence results in an insulted or hurt conclusion: "Jay wouldn't eat my piecrust!" Piecrust was a touchy point in my upbringing. You swallowed it if it killed you; otherwise you implied that it was too tough to chew or something else was the matter with it. What baker could be expected to put up with that? —*the author* (pg. 285)

11. Spelt is a type of flour. (pg. 287)

Sources

Papers, Magazines, and Music CD

_____. *Farmer's and Emigrant's Hand* Book, 1845.

Berggren, Dan. *Mountain Air, Traditional and Original Music of the Adirondacks.*1989, Berggren Music. Sleeping Giant Records.

Eckhof, W. R. "It's Smallest Post Office in the World!" *The Postmasters Advocate*, January 1951. (Reprinted through courtesy of *Utica Daily Press*, Utica, New York.

Johnson, Laura Rinkle. "Recipes Out of the Past." *North Country Life*, Spring 1952.

Kimm, S. C. "Life in Herkimer County Eighty Years Ago." North Country Life, Winter 1954, Spring 1954, Summer 1954.

North Country Life, Spring 1952.

Wood, Genevieve L. "Old North Country Recipes." *North Country Life*, Spring 1947.

Wood, Genevieve L. "Old North Country Recipes." *North Country Life*, Summer 1949.

Wood, Genevieve L. "Old North Country Recipes." *North Country Life*, Spring 1950.

Wood, Genevieve L. "Old North Country Recipes." *North Country Life*, Winter 1951.

Wood, Genevieve L. "Old North Country Recipes." *North Country Life*, Spring 1951.

Books

Beetle, David H. *Up Old Forge Way/West Canada Creek.* North Country Books, 1972.

Jordan II, Gilbert H. editor. *The Collected Works of S. C. Kimm, Educator, Historian, Rhymester & Author.* 2004. (self-published)

O'Hern, William J. *Life With Noah: Stories and Adventures of Richard Smith with Noah John Rondeau.* North Country Books, 1997.

O'Hern, William J. *Adirondack Stories of the Black River Country.* North Country Books, 2003.

O'Hern, William J. *Adirondack Characters and Campfire Yarns.* The Forager Press, 2005.

O'Hern, William J. *Under an Adirondack Influence: The Life of A.L. Byron-Curtiss (1871-1959).* The Forager Press, 2008.

Tissot, Caperton. *Adirondack Ice, A Cultural and Natural History.* Snowy Owl Press, 2010.

ACKNOWLEDGEMENTS

THIS IS THE FIRST historical story-cookbook I've ever attempted. The project would not have been possible without the many contributions of photographs, memories, and recipes that have been generously donated. I would like to give my sincere thanks to all who have helped me develop *Spring Trout & Strawberry Pancakes: Borrowed Tales, Quirky Cures, Camp Recipes and the Adirondack Characters Who Cooked Them Up.*

Special thanks to Roy E. Wires. It was his grandmother Emily Mitchell Wires's Camp Cozy cookbook and photographs that initiated this project.

I extend my gratitude to Debra Kimok, Special Collections Librarian, Plattsburgh, State University of New York for help in obtaining copies of Marjorie Lansing Porter's interview and searching for photographs. Katherine K. Lewis, Director of the Town of Webb Historical Association and Kristy Rubyor, Town of Webb Historical Association Administrative Assistant were extremely helpful both looking for photographs from their association's archives and allowing me to poke through the association's files; Bill Zullo, Hamilton County Historian also combed his county's photographs, contributing images that add to the historical nature of the book.

A very special thanks goes to Mary L. Thomas and Neal Burdick. Mary has been my invaluable second right hand from the onset of the manuscript's development. Mary's sound editorial advice and cooking experience is a proven course for anyone who has a story to tell or recipe to share. She reviewed and edited the initial draft and made valuable construction and creative suggestions as well as last-minute additions that crept in right up to the time of printing.

Neal Burdick edited the final draft. His constructive comments and observations tightened and focused the story, suggesting that much jettisoned historical material and recipes would be perfect for another cookbook project. That project has now been completed.

I would also like to express a sincere thank you to: Nancy P. Best, Jeb Brees, Theresa Z. Cataldo, Linda and Wayne Cripe, Gilbert H. Jordon II, North Elba-Lake Placid Historical Society, Paul Sirtoli, Burt Sperry, John Todd, Capertin Tissot, and Francis Woerpel.

Lastly, I would also like to acknowledge, posthumously, Robert Buell, G. Glyndon Cole, Rev. Byron-Curtiss, Maitland DeSormo, John Ferris, Bill Frenette, Otto Horan Jr., Thomas and Doris Kilbourn, Silas Conrad Kimm, Ernestine Koenig, Harold McNitt, Dorothy Mooney, Winfred "Slim" Murdock, Caroline Nelson, Father McNeill, Marjorie Z. O'Hern, Roselle Putney, Leola Schmelzle, Richard J. Smith, Charles and Claire Sperry, Ethel Tripp, Fredia B. Westfall, Margaret Wilcox, Emily Mitchell Wires, and Ethel S. Zysset.

Any ommission to acknowledge the assistance of anyone who helped with this project is an unintentional oversight.

Drawing by Michael E. O'Hern

Spring Trout & Strawberry Pancakes: Borrowed Tales, Quirky Cures, Camp Recipes

INDEX